Beyond Shame

Beyond Shame

BEYOND SHAME

Creating a Healthy Sex Life on Your Own Terms

MATTHIAS ROBERTS

Fortress Press

Minneapolis

BEYOND SHAME
Creating a Healthy Sex Life on Your Own Terms

Cover image: 109 Abstract Smoke Art, by SparkleStock
Cover design: Matthias Roberts and Lauren Williamson
Author photo: Talitha Bullock & Kyle Larson

Print ISBN: 978-1-5064-5566-2
eBook ISBN: 978-1-5064-5567-9

Author's Note
In accordance with ethical and professional standards, most of the names of the people and locations included in this book have been changed, other than my own name and the names of a few friends and colleagues. Identifying details also have been sufficiently modified to obscure identity. Certain people, including most clients, are amalgamations. Conversations recounted from memory are expressed as dialogue.

Disclaimer
This book is designed to provide accurate and authoritative information in regard to the subject matter covered. By its sale, neither the publisher nor the author is engaged in rendering psychological or other professional services. If expert assistance or counseling is needed, the services of a competent professional should be sought.

Portions of chapter 6, "'Queerness Is Sinful'" have previously appeared in Matthias Roberts, "Personhood, Intimacy, and Relational Flourishing: Implications on Lesbian, Gay, and Bisexual Bodies" (masters thesis, The Seattle School of Theology and Psychology, 2017).

In memory of Rachel Held Evans:
thanks for being my cheerleader.

CONTENTS

FOREWORD

TINA SCHERMER SELLERS, PHD

There are times when an idea has been around for so long we fail to see it clearly or question its validity. Such is the idea that sex is shame filled. How could that which creates life—our very heartbeat, the shared experience of pleasure, family, community, love, life on this planet, and all the possibility of the human experience—be fundamentally shame filled? And yet the deep-seated assumption that sex is shameful continues to create our knee-jerk responses. Why has this belief had such durability? Why has it had us in its grip for so long and continued to rob us of joy?

The answers are simultaneously simple and complex.

We could talk about the mind-body split of the early philosophers, who developed the dualistic idea that the mind is eternal while the body is just a temporal and fading part of us. We could talk about Constantine's church leaders, who adopted the mind-body split and taught that the body is evil and will cause you to turn away from God. We could talk about our more recent Victorian ancestors, who spread their sexual repression and obsession to America, teaching that sex for anything but procreation is impure and evil. Or we could talk about the origins of the Purity Movement in the 1980s and early 1990s, when it was no longer good enough to save yourself for marriage, and in addition to being taught physical restraint, youth were told to keep themselves pure in all thought, all desire, and all action until the day of heterosexual matrimony. Of course, if we wanted to take an even closer look at each of these moments in history, we could find the corrupt stories of power and control, men and money, and the forces of manipulation at work behind each of these scenes. But suffice it to say, the loaded message that came down from person to person, generation to generation, parent to child is this: Any body-curiosity or pleasure desire having to do with genitals (yours or anyone else's) is bad, dirty, and perverted. Curiosity or attraction toward anyone other than someone of the opposite sex, or an experience of gender identity other than that which matches the genitals "assigned to you at birth"—that also is bad, dirty, and perverted.

For two thousand years, this body- and sex-shaming religious culture has primarily privileged those who are white, wealthy, straight, cisgendered, able-bodied, and male. These are and have been the people for whom all doors of leadership are wide open. These have been the decision makers.

As our country has become more diverse, however, and an appreciation for this diversity has grown, more and more people desire to have their churches be representative of the people and communities in their lives. Over the years, as the church has failed to recognize and respond to the desires and needs of its people, the costs have mounted:

- Currently congregants, especially those under forty, are leaving the organized Western church in droves in search of a more authentic experience of faith and worship rooted in love, justice, and diversity. They speak of a genuine hunger for the reunion of spirituality and sexuality, a hunger still being insufficiently addressed by most theologies of white-dominant Western churches. This silence and ignorance breed profound sexual shame and suffering, impacting core identity, attachment, and happiness. Many people—men, women, and queer alike—are seeking to heal from sexual shame and to experience the gift of sexual and spiritual abundance they believe God created them to know.

- Sexual abuse and sexual violence are rampant in the United States (one in three girls and one in five boys will experience sexual violence), with 90 percent of the perpetrators being boys/men in power over those with lesser power. America also has one of the highest teen pregnancy and STI rates of the top fifty industrialized countries. The church has, in large part, failed to provide age-appropriate sex education across the life cycle to equip children, adolescents, young adults, and parents who are desperate for this knowledge. This has left congregants ignorant and vulnerable, without the skills to spot potential danger signs and disempowered in making sexual-health decisions in line with their faith values. I believe the church can speak out about sexual violence; support victims; teach consent and sexuality education; teach sexual responsibility, sexual self-control, and self-discipline to boys (not making girls responsible for boys' sexual behavior); and swiftly support the punishment of sexual perpetrators.

- The eligibility of church members for leadership and ordination without regard to sexual orientation or gender identity continues to be a topic of profound divisiveness and oppression in the church, causing immeasurable pain for LGBTQ+ individuals and their family members and robbing congregations of the spiritual gifts and talents these individuals have to bring to their communities.

The desire for a shame-less, liberated, love- and justice-filled experience of worship and service is completely transforming churches across the country. It is time to flip the script and begin to talk about what we can do to create a shame-free, life-giving, grace-filled culture where we can live the life we were created to live—an abundant life of connection and pleasure.

I was recently reading Stella Resnik's book *Body-to-Body Intimacy*, trying to answer the question "How, physiologically, are we hardwired for connection and pleasure?" Resnik shares Harry Harlow's experiments with monkeys deprived of sex play in their youth. When the young monkeys did not have access to sex play with their peers, they were unable to engage in sexual activity as adult monkeys, because they could not read the mating signals of the partnering monkeys. Now, I realize we are not monkeys, and though we would never subject humans to such experiments, I see the effects of such deprivations in my office all the time!

We know that the right brain of an infant is active to all the senses (touch, sound, taste, hearing, sight) from birth and is taking in emotional information from their caregiver. This connection and pleasure/pain center is forming what will become the emotional foundation for that adult—for better or worse. The left brain (logic) does not become active until language develops at eighteen to twenty-four months. We know from psychobiologist Jaak Pansksepp's research that all forms of childhood play that are free, creative, fun, exploratory, relational, and sensorimotor have an effect on a child's ability to think creatively, solve problems, learn social skills (sex is social), increase physical fitness, and many other positive outcomes. Conversely, many of the couples and individuals presenting clinically with intimacy and sexual issues can recall early experiences of "being caught" or punished for masturbating or "playing doctor" with a playmate and still feel profound shame. This shame is almost always at the heart of their attachment and sexual problems—low desire, sexual secrecy, betrayal, ignorance (lack of knowledge), out-of-control sexual behavior, and sexual dysfunction. Clearly, failing to promote healthy sexuality as part of normal human development is negatively impacting our overall well-being, self-esteem, human attachment, and sexual experience.

On a basic level, human beings are hardwired for connection and pleasure (and averse to isolation and rejection) from the moment we leave the womb. A mountain of research has been done in the field of positive psychology to show that when we feel joy, contentment, and pleasure, we are more likely to expand our thinking, be creative, be playful, connect with others, and reach our goals. The opposite is true when we feel negative emotions, shame being one of them. When we experience shame from our parents, the church, or the society at large, we find our thoughts narrowed, our stress hormones raised, and even our ability to fight disease diminished. Fundamentally, when we feel sexual shame, we feel unworthy of love and belonging from *those we love and from God*. We are profoundly isolated, and we believe we deserve it. To put it simply, shame hurts, and pleasure heals.

If you have been steeped in purity culture or remnants of the Protestant work ethic (or in my case, Scandinavian stoicism), reading "Pleasure heals" may sound somehow extravagant, indulgent, wasteful, or excessive. *However, it is absolutely true.* We know it intuitively when we look in the eyes of children. But somehow, we lose this awareness as we grow into adulthood. We have to overcome a deep socialization—one that tells us that we don't matter, that pleasure doesn't matter, that joy doesn't matter, that rest and self-care don't matter, that taking care of each other doesn't matter, that children separated from their parents don't matter, that working eighty hours a week doesn't matter, that being too busy to plan play time with our partner doesn't matter, that sleep doesn't matter, that nutritious food doesn't matter, that good sex doesn't matter, that black lives don't matter, that LGBTQ+ lives don't matter, that people being poor doesn't matter, that women don't matter. We have been defining love by obligation, by holidays, behind closed doors, by fantasy and social media, by products tied up in plastic that we pile up and throw away, by what *you* can do for *me*.

We are all going to die of loneliness and depression if we keep "loving" from this fake place instead of our heart. Prioritizing deep pleasure and connection—love for ourselves and love for each other—is an act of political and spiritual resistance. It is an act of standing up to religious and sexual shame and claiming God's profound and relentless love. Living out this love becomes an act of radical justice. It's not enough to simply name it; we need to fight for the kind of culture we want and for the kind of church we want.

So, what does this mean? What does a culture of pleasure, connection, and justice look like moving forward? How do we put skin on it? It looks like speaking up. It is not enough to simply name what we want (a shame-free, sexually just future for ourselves and the generations to come); we now have to fight for it, to demand it. Pleasure and connection are what our bodies, our human systems, are created for, what ignites a natural gratitude and humility, the joy and celebration of being a miraculous creation of a loving God. This is the place where body, mind, emotions, and spirit can commune in the holy of holies of God's love. I would argue, as the author of the book in your hands would, that there is no sexual or spiritual health without justice. As Jesus himself said, "I came that they may have life and may have it abundantly" (John 10:10).

Tina Schermer Sellers, PhD
Author of *Sex, God, and the Conservative Church: Erasing Shame from Sexual Intimacy*

INTRODUCTION: DON'T LOOK! SEX, SHAME, AND FAITH

"Cover your eyes, Matt!"

My mom's voice is etched in my memory, prompting an almost automatic response any time I see a Victoria's Secret ad. And I don't even like girls.

That's the first thing I remember learning about sex, "Cover your eyes!" A kiss on TV, a billboard for a sex shop, the Rockettes—as a little boy, I would squeeze my eyes tight, turning my head away, wanting to make sure my mom knew I wasn't looking. Sometimes I would catch her glancing at my dad, making sure he was looking away, too. He wasn't.

I knew from an early age that we should not look at such things. Bodies, flesh, and nakedness—all those were off limits. Dirty. As if even looking at them would somehow make us dirty, too. As if squeezing my eyes tight would delay my inevitable sexual development and my "purity" would remain intact. I'm not sure if my sisters were given the same instruction when shirtless dudes came on TV—I certainly didn't look away—but my parents told them other things. Instead of covering their eyes, they had to cover their bodies. They were given instructions on how to cover themselves to keep their brothers in Christ from stumbling, as if it were all my sisters' responsibility.

How can a young man keep his way pure? By requiring every woman around him to wear a flour sack. "I think girls in long dresses are hotter," a guy in my youth group said. "It leaves more to the imagination." I nodded along, as if I knew what he was talking about.

One of the most recognizable markers of shame is turning away: covering your eyes, turning your face, saying to the world, "I don't want you to look at me, and I don't want to look at you." Here's a fundamental truth: shame makes us turn away. When we feel its flush, we automatically look down, or to the nearest exit, or anywhere but toward its source. We seek to cover ourselves and put as much distance as possible between the shame and us, especially if we're in the presence of other people. I was taught to have these same reactions when a woman wearing a swimsuit appeared on a billboard.

Years later, I realized how troubling it was that I was taught to respond to seeing a woman's body in a way that mimics the classic expression of shame. It wasn't a natural response. I remember being confused and sometimes yelling back at my mom, "Why?!" It made no sense to me that I shouldn't look at people's bodies, but the aversion of my eyes gradually became involuntary.

By the time I started sneaking off to the men's underwear aisle in Walmart, a shame response was already ingrained in me. I would keep my eyes down on the way there, not even glancing at the bras, imagining that if I were to make eye contact with a woman shopping in that section, she'd loudly scold, just like my mom: "Don't look! Close your eyes!" But when I reached the men's section, I'd slowly bring my eyes up and stare at all the models with curiosity and desire.

One day when I was around eleven years old, studying the man on a five-pack of Fruit of the Loom boxer briefs, it clicked: this is what other guys feel for women. This is why I wasn't supposed to look at them. These feelings, the beginnings of my conscious sexuality, were emerging, and I knew this was what my parents were trying to teach me how to control. I felt dirty—doubly so because on the heels of that realization, I recognized I wasn't even feeling the right kind of dirty feelings. Instead of directing my curiosity and longing toward women as I was supposed to, everything was focused on guys.

I began to avert my eyes from men's bodies too, but I found it to be much more difficult. I kept sneaking glances, returning for a longing look that I'm sure my mom caught a time or two. In the aisles of T-shirts and boxers, I began to go to war with my body.

SEXUALITY AND SHAME

With all the attention shame has gotten in the past decade, it doesn't take a shame expert to draw connections between sex, sexuality, and shame. We know it deeply, in our bodies. Even for people who grew up in more sex-positive homes than mine, or who have done incredible amounts of work around their sexuality and sex lives, the connection is hard to escape. Wherever there is sex, there seems to be shame.

Sometimes sexual shame is overt. Think, for example, of people who grew up saving sex for marriage only to be overwhelmed on their wedding night by debilitating shame, preventing all the parts from working right. Sometimes, the shame is more subtle. I had a professor once who described the bedroom as the "noisiest place in the house."[1] All the voices of who we are and who we are not, the voices of people we've slept with in the past, our parents, the bullies on the playground, and the random guy who shouted that one thing on the street the other day—they all try to take up space the moment we hit the bed. Sometimes we're good at ignoring those voices, and sometimes we aren't.

Sex and shame have been linked to one another in psychological literature since the beginning of psychology; they're inseparable. With the profound beauty and goodness of sexual relationships comes the potential for shame to hijack that beauty and goodness, as if it's part of our human nature.

Many of us can navigate our sexual shame reasonably well. Our defense mechanisms are sufficient to keep shame from becoming debilitating, and we proceed as usual, hardly even noticing it. But our sexuality and our sex lives are a microcosm of the rest of our lives. What shows up in our daily lives will show up in the bedroom, and vice versa. And wherever shame is unrecognized, it's because we've constructed some barriers to keep ourselves from feeling it.

We need to learn how to recognize shame and bring it into the light. As that happens, we're able to untangle ourselves from the effects of shame, leading not only to better sex lives, but also to better lives in general.

DEFINING SEX AND SEXUALITY

Let's begin by defining what I mean when I talk about sex and sexuality. First, I believe that sexuality exists at the very core of who we are. It is an inescapable part of our identity. Christian orthodoxy has long recognized that we cannot split sexuality off from who we are as people, even though modern Christians often try to separate sexual orientation—particularly sexual orientations that fall outside of norms—and claim it can be isolated from the rest of our sexuality. Make no mistake about it: our sexuality is an essential part of us, including those who identify as bisexual, lesbian, queer, and gay.[2]

Sex and sexuality are not synonyms. When I refer to

sex, I'm talking about a physical act, defined as broadly or narrowly as you like. In no part of this book will I attempt to define what physical sex is and isn't. Too many people have already done that while trying to regulate others' behavior, which has resulted in considerable damage. I'm not interested in drawing those kinds of lines.

Sexuality, however, is broader. It is what gives birth to the physicality of sex and comprises a vast number of elements, including but not limited to our sexual and romantic orientations. I know this description is vague, and that is both beneficial and frustrating. These distinctions will become more evident as we work with them in the chapters that follow. My goal throughout is not to say this is what sex and sexuality are and aren't. I'm offering a framework that will function regardless of how you define these terms for yourself.

The distinction between sex and sexuality will be familiar to people who have spent any time in conversations about sexuality in Christian churches. We see this distinction in Scripture, especially in Jesus's Sermon on the Mount in Matthew 5, where Jesus acknowledges both our internal sexual worlds and our external actions. Some Christians have used this distinction to make the argument that your sexuality itself isn't sinful, but sex and any kind of sexual thoughts are. In this way, faith communities have weaponized these definitions, both in shaping purity culture and in attacking LGBTQ people. The distinction between sex and sexuality has been used to enforce celibacy and to regulate who can and cannot have sex, and in what contexts.

I want to be clear up front: In exploring the ideas and practices around shame in this book, I have no interest in policing sex or sexuality, because I know how deeply harmful that can be. What I am doing is offering loose definitions of sex and sexuality that will serve us in the discussion going forward, and I take an expansive and inclusive view. Sex is an outflowing of sexuality that is connected to an event, and sexuality is a broad and flowing energy linked to our emotional, physical, intellectual, and spiritual identities.

I write most often in this book about people who experience sexual desire, but I want to note that one's lack of sexual or romantic desire can also fill this identity-construing space. For our asexual and aromantic siblings, a lack of sexual and/or romantic drive is just as significant in terms of defining identity as sexual desire is for those of us who experience it. Too often when we argue that sexuality exists at the core of our personhood, our language excludes an entire group of people who don't experience sexuality or romantic connections. The implicit assumption is that those who don't experience these things or who experience these things differently than we do don't have personhood. This is not the case. We can learn much about personhood and relationship from our siblings who move through the world differently than the majority.

DEFINING SHAME

Shame is a buzzword these days, thanks to the work that researcher and storyteller Brené Brown has done to bring it into the cultural spotlight. My therapy colleagues and I talk about shame a *lot*, but I notice it come up in conversations among non-therapists all over the place when I travel. Just as discussions about shame seem to be everywhere, shame itself is everywhere.

Brené Brown makes a distinction between shame and guilt,[3] which is a helpful way to get to a working definition of shame. When we do something we're not proud of, the voice of guilt says, "I *did* something wrong/bad/I'm not proud of," but the voice of shame says, "I *am* something wrong/bad/I'm not proud of."

Voices of shame construe identity; they tell us stories about who we are as people, who we are at our core. They're the voices that make us want to hide and turn away. They make us want to disconnect from the world, and they scare us into thinking we're not worthy of connection anyway. They tell us we are too much and not enough, often both at the same time. Our shame voices tap into our fears and the sense of powerlessness they bring. They say, "This is the way things will always be"; "I'm not strong enough to be able to change this"; and "I can't stop this from happening."

Several years ago, I was scrolling through my Instagram feed and stumbled across a photo an ex posted with a new significant other, posing in front of a sign that said "Love" (or something just as nauseating). I was still feeling the sting of heartbreak and was caught off guard to see that they had moved on so quickly. Immediately, I began to notice biological responses: my face flushed, my heart started beating faster, my vision blurred and tunneled, and my chest constricted. As I stared at that photo, shocked, my shame voices went to work, and my body was working, too. I suddenly felt powerless next to this new guy. I felt in my bones there was something fundamentally wrong with me. There was something this guy had that I didn't. He was loved; I was not. In that moment, I felt I would *never* be loved.

Our shame voices get all jumbled up and mixed with biological responses, creating so much discomfort that we'll do almost anything to escape them. We turn to our favorite numbing activities: food, alcohol, sex. In this way, shame is also anticipatory—we anticipate feeling shame and often adjust our behaviors to avoid experiencing that shame. Where guilt produces a desire to restore something that has gone wrong, shame makes us want to run away and hide.

The voice of shame also tends to be a bit dramatic. It takes things to extremes. When I'm in bed, eating a pizza because I've had a hard week, the voice of shame tells me that I'm a disgusting slob. While there's certainly nothing wrong with eating an entire pizza in bed (other than waking up in the middle of the night with pizza sweats), shame turns that single behavior into a whole narrative about who I am.

Our shame voices sometimes come from inside us and sometimes from others. Often they sound a lot like our parents, and they always result in a bodily response. It can be subtle or overt, but shame always involves our entire bodies, making us feel small and powerless in its grasp. It's a neuro-affective response, which means it involves our minds (our neurology), our physical bodies, and our emotions (which make up our affect). We can't define shame neatly as thought process or physical feeling or emotion; it's all those things at once. And we are likely to do anything to get away from that feeling.

Shame is most easily recognizable when it's a loud, overly dramatic voice. But it also shows up in much smaller ways we don't quickly recognize. It's present in the shoulds and shouldn'ts in our lives, those times we drive by a billboard and think, "I should look like that," or when we suddenly remember the time we said that one thing to that one person and feel the warm flush of "I'm such an idiot." Shame is everywhere and shows up in our lives regularly.

The things we do to avoid the sense of shame are our *coping mechanisms*, or our best attempts to work with all the complicated emotions and thoughts that shame brings up. Sometimes we mistake our coping mechanisms for healthy functioning, and that's when things get tricky, especially when it comes to sexuality.

Several years ago, I attended a lecture series by a shame researcher named Curt Thompson, who told us about keeping a shame journal in which he makes a little tally mark every single time he notices himself feeling shame. I decided to try this, too, and spent the next few days constantly pulling out my phone to mark down every time I felt shame. Over a day, I noticed subtle shame hundreds of times, so often that it felt impractical for me to keep the practice going for more than a couple of days.

Dr. Thompson created a shame journal because one of the first steps in fighting shame is to practice recognizing it. Making a single quick mark interrupts the neuropathways just enough for other parts of ourselves to come online. Ultimately, a journal is a very good starting point, but as this book will demonstrate, shame fighting cannot happen without the presence of other people. We simply can't fight shame alone. For Dr. Thompson and for me, making a tally mark every time we feel shame is an embodied way to practice recognition—a way to begin stopping shame in its tracks.

I'm not suggesting that we all go out and keep shame journals, although it's a practice I often recommend to my clients. More importantly, I am making the point that shame is pervasive. It follows us everywhere we go and shows up more often than we're usually aware. Like all emotions, shame exists on a physical level, and we feel it before our brains even recognize it.

Modern neuroscience confirms that our brains are organized around emotion and not the other way around; we feel things before we think them. Any attempt to control emotions through our cognitive abilities is a futile battle, and it would serve us better to become more aware of our bodies and the emotions that drive us, instead of actively trying to change them. At the end of the book, I've listed some resources that offer a deep dive into the science behind all this. For our purposes, it's enough to know that by the time we've noticed shame, it has already occurred in our bodies.

WHY A BOOK ABOUT SEXUAL SHAME?

This brings me to why I've written this book. All shame is insidious, but I believe that sexual shame holds a special significance. Shame targets the very core of who we are, and the ways we experience sexuality also exist in those core places. This is why sexual shame can feel so debilitating and how it can have such far-reaching effects in our lives.

If we're told that the ways we are wired to experience love and connection and belonging are wrong, that belief has an impact on all the most important areas of our lives. If we're taught from an early age that sex is bad, then we believe our sexual drives must be bad, too. If our sexual drives are bad, and if we find that we can't control them (we can't), then there must be something fundamentally wrong with us. Shame runs freely in these spaces. We begin to split ourselves off, finding ways to manage both our sexual drives and the shame that comes with experiencing them. Things get incredibly unhealthy quickly. Sexual shame ruins us.

I wrote this book because I believe it's important to move beyond shame to a healthier, more life-affirming view of sex and sexuality, especially in our faith communities. Sexuality is tied intimately to who we are as people, and it influences almost every single aspect of our lives. If shame can establish a stronghold within our sexuality, it can do a pretty good job of mucking up our lives. Shame thrives in secrecy, and since many faith communities shun discussions of sexuality except in quiet spaces behind closed doors, sexual shame has been able to grow exponentially in the lives of many people I know.

In our faith communities, more and more people are waking up to the harms of purity culture, and many of us suffer from overwhelming shame around our sex lives or lack of sex lives. We don't know what we're doing, and we feel shame about that. Or we do know what we're doing, and we've been told that because we have sexual experience, no one will love us, and we feel shame about that. We feel shame about the people we're attracted to and when. We feel shame day in and day out, and it seems no one is talking about it, leaving us all alone to try to figure things out.

Perhaps most deeply troubling to me is the fact that so many of us don't know what we believe about sex. We've probably been told that having sex before marriage will literally ruin our lives, yet many of us, after having sex with someone, wake up wondering, "What was so wrong about that?" We believe that we should feel shame at moments when we don't. And we suspect that maybe we shouldn't feel shame when we do. This book is for all of us.

I've spent the past five years talking to people about sex and sexuality, and I've found some common themes. Many of us believe that there is a healthy way to express our sexuality. We can also see that there are unhealthy ways, some of which we may have experienced. But we're deeply uncomfortable with the moralistic categories that our faith communities often use to define sex. Too many people have tried to regulate our sexuality and sex lives with categories of "sin," yet we can't quite shake the feeling that there's something about sex that is, at the very least, worth thinking about deeply.

I see many clients and friends who feel they have to figure things out all by themselves because they don't know where to turn. The truth is that people get weird during conversations about sex. We feel *so much shame*, and we don't know what to do with it.

This book is a place you can bring your shame, and we can think about it together.

When it comes to dealing with sexual shame, I've observed three main ways we attempt to work with it. As I discuss in part 1, we (1) let it rule our lives as shamefulness;[4] (2) completely ignore it, trying to live in shamelessness; or (3) just kind of stumble along somewhere in the middle, on autopilot. Most of us flow among these three responses. Like gender and sexual orientation, our shame responses are fluid. You'll probably recognize yourself in each of those chapters, but these responses aren't meant to serve as ways to "type" ourselves, even though most of us tend to fall into one category most of the time.

The chapters in part 2 look closely at the lies we tell ourselves and the lies the larger society—including the church—tells us about sex and sexuality. We'll look at scripture, gender hierarchy, queer sexuality, and many of the things we were taught as we grew up in Christian and US culture. Regardless of what we now think of Christianity and the Bible, many of these lies inform the particular shape our sexual shame takes. For us to work with our shame, we must wrestle with what we were taught.

And in part 3, I examine the paradoxes at the heart of understanding sex and sexuality so that we can move beyond shame. Much of our shame comes from approaching sex and sexuality as if they're black-and-white concepts. They're not. We're going to dive into the reality that sexuality is filled with paradoxes. As we grasp these paradoxes, they have an impact on how we navigate these complicated waters and provide a path forward.

When we become more familiar with the shape our sexual shame takes, we're able to recognize better what parts of ourselves we've constructed in response to shame. Then, as we work and heal those parts, we can be guided by our values instead of being controlled by our shame. This allows us to experience freedom; it enables us to live our lives and move through the complex world that is sex and sexuality.

I don't pretend to know what your values are, and my goal in these pages is not to try to impose values; that's your work to do. As you make your way through this book, you might find it helpful to talk to someone—a trusted mentor or friend, a therapist, or your journal—about the feelings that are coming up for you.

Ultimately, what we're moving toward is a life lived abundantly *beyond* shame. Instead of covering our eyes and hiding from everything sexual, we will learn to stop turning away from our bodies, our sexuality, and our feelings, and turn toward knowing ourselves and finding freedom. I hope that by doing this work, we can come closer to embracing the abundant life Jesus came to give us—not a life defined by rules and moralistic requirements, but a life that is genuinely life-giving.

Notes

1. This professor is Dr. Dan Allender, a brilliant therapist who has spent his life working with sexual shame, among other things.

2. You may notice here the absence of transgender people from the common "LGBTQ" grouping. This is because I'm specifically talking about sexuality, not gender identity. While many of the concepts in this book may apply to transgender folxs, it's important to distinguish sexual identity from gender identity. They are two different things, and we can't always group them together.

3. Brené Brown, "Listening to Shame," filmed March 2012 in Long Beach, CA, TED video, 20:31, https://tinyurl.com/ngtbqqp.

4. I also owe the genesis of my thinking around these first two categories—shaming vs. shamelessness—to Dr. Dan Allender. While I've introduced my own nuance and research into these categories, which depart from Allender's work, the original naming of these categories comes from him. To hear a brief discussion of these categories (outside of the realm of sexuality) from Allender's perspective, see Dan Allender and Rachael Clinton, "Authenticity and Humility: The Binds of Leadership, Part 3," *The Allender Center Podcast*, July 2, 2016, https://tinyurl.com/y5er86vu.

PART I.

HOW WE COPE WITH SEX
AND SHAME

CHAPTER 1.

SHAMEFULNESS

Many of us who grew up in conservative faith communities were surrounded by sexual shame from the start. We grew up in homes with parents who were afraid to talk about sex or who made any conversations about sex super awkward. We were taught to "bounce our eyes" or to wear below-the-knee skirts. For those of us who grew up in what we now call purity culture, sex was always shrouded in mystery, described only as something reserved for marriage. Maybe we were given a couple of books about growing up and managing our changing bodies, or maybe our parents sat us down for "the talk," but sex was generally an off-limits topic. So our own sexuality became off-limits, too. Or maybe not.

Shame can manifest in vastly different ways, depending on how we're coping. Some of us cut ourselves off from sex and sexuality completely: "I'm not going to experience anything sexual until I'm married." Others engage in sexual expression, but in secret, leading a double life. What unites these seemingly opposite ends of the spectrum is a consistent pattern of secrecy and avoidance. When everything that even has a *hint* of sexuality is met with feelings of shame, those of us who are in this space avoid those feelings until we can't avoid them anymore. We push them down and box them off. Or we indulge in secret, which is its own kind of avoidance. There's rarely any enjoyment beyond momentary pleasure before the shame returns.

Travis, a friend of mine, describes being stuck at one end of this spectrum and not even knowing it. When he was twenty-two, he moved to Los Angeles and was excited to start meeting more gay people, because where he grew up in a rural part of the South, he barely knew any. A few months after the move, he attended a conference called the Gay Christian Network in Portland—an event he thought would feel safe and familiar, given his Christian upbringing. "I assumed that anyone who called themselves 'Christian' held to a rigorous sexual ethic, but as the conference went on, I realized that many of the participants there were having sex all the time."

Travis was shocked. "If I'd had pearls, I would have clutched them." He described sitting near the convention center café on the second day of the conference and writing in his journal, "I think people here are having sex, and my heart feels so burdened by this." He elaborated, "I thought the Holy Spirit was convicting me, but instead, I was coming face-to-face with the impact of the culture of shame in which I had been raised."

Of course, Travis had encountered sexually active people before, even when he was in high school, but he told me about easily dismissing that behavior by telling himself, "Oh, they're not Christians." His moralistic code could handle that split pretty easily, but he was suddenly surrounded by thousands of Christians who were having sex even when they weren't married. Travis didn't have categories for this, and he didn't know how to reconcile what seemed like such a contradiction in his mind.

More importantly, Travis didn't know that the culture of shame he had grown up in had influenced his views of healthy sexuality so much. "I sat in that room and judged everyone around me, viewing them with suspicion, asking the question, 'How in the world can they call themselves Christians?' I had been taught that our Christian identity hinges upon right sexuality, right sexual expression." Travis had done the work to accept and embrace his own sexual orientation as fitting into the category of "right sexuality," but he did not yet recognize how deeply his attitudes were shaped by the sexual shame that surrounded him his entire life.

COPING WITH SHAMEFULNESS

One way to cope with our shame is to let it take control. I call this coping mechanism "shamefulness." When everything we do is permeated by shame, we are shame-full in every sense of the word. Shamefulness is based on the presupposition there is a "right" context for sexual expression and a "wrong" context for it. Any sexual activity outside of that context (whether defined by marriage, commitment, the gender of the person we desire, or other criteria) is deemed bad or wrong.

When we are taught the "right" context for sexual expression, at some point many of us discover that our sexuality, our sexual desire, and our fantasy lives don't exactly fit into such a neat box. We learn that we will have to struggle against our desires. If sex outside of the prescribed context is bad, it would seem to follow that our desire to have sex outside of that context also must be bad. Now we feel dirty, and we can't shake the feeling that there's something wrong with us for desiring sex outside of the right context. This is the voice of shame telling us loud and clear, "I am dirty and bad because I want something dirty and bad."

Internalizing our shame, we work to take every thought captive. We start building elaborate rules, strategies, and methods of accountability to eradicate any sexual thought or feeling that falls outside of the proper context. Sometimes the rules, strategies, and accountability techniques work, but most often they don't. We mess up.

Messing up intensifies our shame, leading us to believe that we are even worse than before. We believe we don't have enough self-control, or we're not trying hard enough, or we aren't good enough. We believe our sexual feelings and thoughts are too much. We heap new shame on top of our already existing shame.

We double down on our attempts to control our feelings, establishing more rules and more strategies. This creates a vicious cycle. Shame rules.

"Messing up" is what Isaac and Lionel called it any time they watched porn or masturbated as undergraduates. Isaac, a man in his early thirties, met me in a small coffee shop while I was visiting North Carolina for a conference. His large frame would have been intimidating if not for his quick smile.

While sipping a latte, Isaac described going to a big college and getting involved in a campus ministry. It was there where he met Lionel, who quickly became one of his best friends.

Late one night as they sat studying, said Isaac, Lionel blurted out, "I think I need an accountability partner." Isaac said he stopped what he was doing and looked at him, intrigued but feeling a bit of panic, knowing what he was about to say.

Lionel continued, "I've been masturbating more and more, and I need to stop." Isaac told me he sat in silence, feeling super awkward. Thankfully, they were in Lionel's dorm room, so no one else would hear their conversation, but until this point, Isaac and Lionel hadn't had the kind of relationship that would warrant Lionel's bluntness.

Even so, Isaac sensed he could be honest. And, without looking at Lionel, Isaac whispered, "Me, too."

As he continued his story, Isaac recalled that he and Lionel spent the next few hours confessing their sins to each other, which was a relief because neither of them had ever been able to talk openly about sex and sexuality before. Isaac had never talked to anyone about the fact that he masturbated. He and Lionel made a pact that night to check in with each other every day. They installed software on their computers that would send reports to the other if it caught one of them on porn sites. And they agreed to keep track of how many times they masturbated each week, meeting every Saturday afternoon to go for a walk far away from campus to compare notes.

Isaac described how incredible it felt to have a friend he could be open with. He said that he and Lionel would set goals like "I'm going to go for an entire month without masturbating." And whenever they failed, which they always did, it felt good not to have to carry the shame alone. They were trying so hard, so earnestly, to live up to a standard that told them to avoid even sexual thoughts.

One night about a year later, Isaac continued, Lionel got really quiet. He had recently started dating a girl he had a massive crush on. Isaac remembers that night well: Lionel looked at him and admitted, "She gave me a hand job in the back seat of the car the other night." Isaac met his eyes with shock. Lionel went on to admit to several other sexual experiences he'd had over the previous year that he hadn't told Isaac about, being careful to assure Isaac that he hadn't actually had *sex*.

I asked Isaac what "actual sex" meant for him and Lionel. He told me, "Oh, you know, basically anything outside of vaginal penetration wasn't actually sex. We called it other things. But," he continued, "I thought

Lionel and I had given up all of that. I certainly wasn't doing any of that with my girlfriend at the time."

Isaac described his reaction to the incident: "I was pissed. Why hadn't he told me? We were both on leadership in our campus ministry, and all of a sudden, I felt like I didn't know Lionel at all. That wasn't how we were supposed to act. I muttered something about God forgiving sin—blah, blah, blah—and we went on to renew our pact with each other once again." In Isaac's view, Lionel seemed genuinely sorry, and he promised Isaac that he was going to stop. The two friends got even more specific about ways they would pray for each other and hold each other accountable. They made a plan for what he would do if he found himself getting aroused while with his girlfriend. He would text Isaac, and Isaac promised to "cockblock him" by rushing over to his room or by calling and inviting them to come do something.

As Isaac described his reaction and the promises made, he told me, "It all seems so weird now, looking back." Yet, continued Isaac, the friends' strategy didn't work. Lionel never texted in the moment. And even though Isaac's own masturbation habits never actually changed, he started feeling superior to Lionel, "because at least I wasn't getting physical with another person."

As Isaac was feeling self-righteous, he didn't understand that they both were coping by adopting a posture of shamefulness. Neither young man was living in freedom; shame was ruling every aspect of their sexuality. Isaac said later in our conversation, "We had no concept of sexual freedom, or perhaps we believed that freedom was for some future point in our lives. As twentysomethings, our sexual drives were burdens we had to endure and control until we were finally in the right context." For Lionel, that context was marriage, which Isaac told me Lionel accomplished rather quickly after they graduated.

For Isaac, however, rushing to get married wasn't in the cards. He broke up with his girlfriend during his senior year and is still looking for the right woman. He told me, "I started thinking of my own sexuality as 'my cross to bear' and 'a thorn in my flesh.'"

As I listened to Isaac, I imagined thinking about his sexuality in those terms felt good because he was coping through shamefulness. His story certainly reminded me of all the messages I was told about sexuality. Isaac readily admitted that his attitude also illustrates how much less connected to his body he was than Lionel was to his. "Throughout college," he explained to me, "I would wrap myself up in fantasies almost every day, keeping my sexual expression inside my head, while Lionel acted his out in backseats and dorm rooms."

Regardless of how their sexuality expressed itself physically, the result for both Isaac and Lionel was *more* shame. In Isaac's words, "We both were 'messing up,' and despite every new strategy we tried, every new book we studied together, we couldn't gain mastery over our sexual desires."

If we grow up surrounded by sexual shame, in environments where sex is shrouded in secrecy and framed in terms of "Don't do this" or "Don't get too close to the line," we internalize that shame. Shamefulness as a coping mechanism is the most obvious sign of that internalized shame. Because we've been taught that having sex is bad outside of a certain context, we decide that in order to be "good," we're not going to have sex or engage in anything remotely sexual. We become hypervigilant in our attempts to control what we think about, what we watch, what we pay attention to. This is how Isaac was living. If we discover that we can't *not* have sex, and we can't *not* think about sex and sexuality, we will certainly hate ourselves when we "act out" and break our own rules in secrecy, as Lionel did. The two behavior patterns are both sides of the same coin.

LIVING DOUBLE LIVES

One of my clients, Leon, grew up in a small town in Texas. He was taught a strict moral code—a code that, on the surface, he appeared to follow well. He was a worship leader and spent much of his time at the church. But when he wasn't at church, he was in another culture, participating in night after night of hookups, risky sex, and secretive encounters that put both him and his sexual partners in danger. He lived a double life and is still, years later, working through the effects that had on him. In one of our first sessions together, he described to me all the fear he lived in, worrying about what would happen if someone in his church were to run into him at a club or some morning after one of his hookups.

Almost all of us who use shamefulness as a coping mechanism know the feeling Leon describes. The sense of dread arises, as we think, "If these people actually knew what was going on behind the scenes. . . ." Some of us are successful at living seemingly ascetic lives, but our sexuality still often manifests in one way or another, either alone in our bedrooms or with others behind closed doors.

Control, avoidance, and secrecy are the critical tools of shamefulness. When we're deep in the waters of shamefulness, we usually cope by trying to control the shame by controlling our sexuality. We think that by setting up systems, trying hard enough, and having enough willpower, we can avoid sexual experiences and our sexuality until we find ourselves in the correct context. If we discover we can't avoid sexual experiences, we cover them up in webs of secrecy. We tell ourselves one thing but do another. We lead double lives, often lying to ourselves as frequently as we lie to others.

Shamefulness manifests itself in any number of ways, and its fingerprints can be found all over the walls of our churches and faith communities. It is what lurks behind so many scandals and so much harm that gets swept under the rugs to maintain and preserve images. I wish we understood that this harm is completely avoidable, but that understanding would require us to change the way we interact with our sexuality. It would require us pulling up the rugs and looking frankly at the messages we're preaching about sexuality. Sexuality is not something we need to fight against. When we do fight against it, when we fight against ourselves, we usually wind up deep in the murky waters of shame, living double lives, just trying to cope.

THE FIERY CANYON OF SEXUALITY

I remember growing up in church and hearing the gospel presented every week. If you didn't experience this, let me help you imagine it: You're three or four years old and graduating from the nursery to the first level of Sunday school—a whole hour of coloring and stories! Or maybe, instead of Sunday school, your parents sent you to AWANA, a Bible memorization club that coaxed you with snacks and crafts and game time. This was much more fun than Sunday school, which was usually taught by sweet older ladies who couldn't hear very well. Or maybe you went to church camp, or Good News Club, or vacation Bible school—an entire week during the summer with fun themes (pirates! space!), snacks, and games—a general delight. If you're like me, you were sent to each of these at some point. In every case, from age three to age twelve, you would sit down after some play time with a full tummy to hear the good news.

The sharing of the gospel usually followed a simple trajectory:

1. You're a terrible person, and nothing you can ever do will change that.

2. But that's OK, because Jesus was brutally murdered.

3. But then he came back to life!

4. So now, all you need to do is admit that you're an unlovable piece of dirt and accept Jesus into your heart by praying a three-sentence prayer.

This explanation of the gospel was terrifying and comforting all at the same time, and the thing is, it worked!

As I got older, each point was described in more theologically sophisticated ways, especially the first point: we are all terrible people, and nothing we can do will ever change that. In one particularly memorable metaphor, we were shown a picture of a vast canyon with a tiny little person standing on one side looking forlornly across the gap at what we were told was heaven. In case the drama wasn't perfectly apparent, the canyon was full of flames and suffering people. We were told to imagine trying to jump across the canyon. Surely we'd fall into the flames. We were told to imagine that we were older and better at jumping. Still we'd be burned by the flames, but maybe we'd make it a little farther across the abyss. Then we were told to imagine that we were Olympic pole vaulters. But that would just get us even deeper into the flames. Finally, instead of suggesting a helicopter, which would have been my first thought, the Sunday school teacher would plop a giant cross on the picture—a makeshift bridge—and we'd understand that we could all safely walk across to the sound of the Olympians' screams below.

The imagery was clear. No matter how hard we tried, no matter how much effort we put into it, no matter how much training we went through, no matter how many times we shared our snacks or let girls come into our Only Boys Allowed blanket forts, no matter how many times we said "please," there was *nothing* we could do on our own to bridge that canyon. We needed something else. We needed the bridge of the cross and Jesus's love. No helicopter was going to show up. For children, this simple imagery worked and is forever etched into many of our memories.

The problem is that our faith communities still seem to approach teachings and practices around adult sexuality as if we were training to jump across a fiery canyon. Instead of heaven, we see "sexual freedom and happiness" on the other side of the canyon, all within the bounds of a specific "right" context. But we wonder where the bridge is. In our real lives, we are left trying to jump across without a bridge in sight, falling again and again into the flames of shame. Some of us attempt to build a bridge the way Lionel did, by getting married as young as possible, so we don't have to "burn with passion." But for most of us, this doesn't seem to help. Shame still permeates our sexuality, and all our techniques don't work; they leave us falling into the chasm. We're left picking up the pieces, hating ourselves even more, begging God to release us from our sinful flesh, and looking for yet another strategy. At some point, we probably give up, accepting that we will always fail and living out our sexual lives plagued by shame and secrecy.

As problematic as the flaming-canyon metaphor is, there's a fundamental truth in it. We can't just "try harder." Trying harder doesn't get us anywhere. In fact, if we continue with this illustration, trying harder actually only manages to push us *deeper* into the gorge. It only propels us further into shame. Anytime we use the tools of control and avoidance to manage anything, especially our sexuality, we end up falling deeper in the muck. Most of us know this from experience.

We fear that the alternative to trying harder to reach our goal of an ideal healthy sexuality is complete chaos. We fear that if we let go of our attempts to squeeze ourselves into boxes of rules and regulations, we'll tailspin into a valueless life of debauchery. Many of us even hold tightly to our shame, claiming that it keeps us healthy, on the straight and narrow, and safe.

Living in sexual freedom sounds terrifying if we are stuck in shamefulness, because we can't imagine what freedom looks like. We fear that it may mean giving up some of our core values. We may actually want to abstain from sex until marriage or to stop using porn.

There is a way out of this dilemma, a way across the chasm of shame into a world of sexual freedom that is deeply rooted in our values, whatever they may be. The other side of that chasm is a place where we can stand on our values and operate from a sturdy ground of authenticity, not feeling a need to control, avoid, or hide our sexuality. Shame may still haunt us sometimes, but we can learn how to work with it and how to fight it.

CHAPTER 2.

SHAMELESSNESS

Hannah came into our therapy session pissed. She had been looking around at her life, and it seemed like everyone but her was having massive amounts of sex. "They're either casually hooking up or in happy, committed relationships," she reported to me with an eye roll. "Everyone seems so blissful."

Hannah was swimming in resentment around her lack of a sex life, a topic that had been coming up again and again over the last few weeks. She told me about her hairstylist sharing stories of her night and about her friends who talked often about the people they had hooked up with recently. To top it all off, her best friend had just gotten into a new relationship. It seemed like every person she passed by on the street was living a sexually liberated life of delight and pleasure. And she was over it.

Hannah and I had been working together for some time, so I felt fairly comfortable with the words I said next, knowing how her shame was keeping her from exploring anything at all: "Maybe it's time for you to make a few mistakes?"

She rolled her eyes. "That doesn't sound like good advice."

But to my surprise, within a week, Hannah was dating

a girl she described to me as "cute enough." It was the first date she had ever told me about, and she hadn't just gone out once with this girl. They had spent the entire weekend together, too. It seemed like my words had become a battle cry.

Over the next few weeks, Hannah's relationship with Mistake Girl, as she later called her, burned fast. Hannah had never been in an actual relationship in her twenty-four years and was eager to get all of her firsts out of the way, to be just like all the people around her: her first time being greeted at the door with flowers, her first kiss, and her first time having sex. Hannah jumped into it all, keeping me updated along the way. She was excited but also couldn't shake the feeling that something wasn't quite right. She was doing all the things that she had wanted to do for so long, but for some reason, they didn't actually feel good to her.

Eventually, some of us get so fed up with the shame around our sexuality that we are ready to just move on with our lives. We declare one morning, "You know what, I'm not going to feel this shame anymore." We push it aside and jump into newfound freedom, just like that. This is the coping mechanism of shamelessness.

Even if we haven't been able to put our feelings into words, we know what shame feels like—every corner of the boxes we tried to contort ourselves into. At some point, a switch is thrown, and we're over it. We're done with shame. Our turn from shamefulness to shamelessness might involve coming out or leaving a toxic church environment. It might happen in a yoga class during Corpse Pose. However it happens, the result is the same: we decide that instead of shame controlling us, we're going to control it.

We attempt to control shame the best way we know how: casting off all the rules, all the boxes, all the voices telling us how to live our lives. They don't apply to us anymore, because they're remnants of our old selves and of old-fashioned ways of living. "I'm sorry," we say, "the old me can't come to the phone right now."

Some of us tiptoe in, and some of us jump in headfirst. We do all the things we've wanted to do (or maybe have already been secretly doing), and we do them boldly. It's great at first, but there is often a nagging sense of . . . something in the background. When we're honest with ourselves, we can admit that we don't exactly feel free; we just feel like we're running away.

We will all go through (and return to) periods of shamelessness at some point in our lives. It's a method of self-correction, or overcorrection—a pendulum swing. It's the "Fuck it all, I'm gonna live my life" attitude. And it's perfectly normal.

However, shamelessness is not really an escape from shame. When we choose shamelessness, we *insist* we're shameless. But somewhere underneath, there's a nagging sense that if we slow down long enough or think too hard about what we're doing, we'll get sucked back in. We're worried shame might just be waiting around the next corner to envelop us.

In embracing shamelessness, we have two options: we can acknowledge the shame and learn to work with it, or we can build elaborate defenses to protect ourselves from it. The first option is the real way out, but many of us get stuck in option two indefinitely, becoming better and better at ignoring the shame that's lurking, but never entirely leaving it behind.

GIVING UP SHAME FOR LENT

Last year, my client Jon walked into my office, sat down on my couch, and proclaimed, "I'm giving up shame and insecurity for Lent." Lent is the period of forty days leading up to Easter and is observed by many Christian denominations as a time of repentance and self-denial as a way of symbolizing and participating in the suffering of Jesus. Many Christians choose to give up something for Lent—chocolate, gossip, social media—something that will produce suffering. Then we spend the next forty days telling everyone about it.

Jon hadn't planned on giving up anything. He had skipped the Ash Wednesday church service, which marks the first day of Lent, although the service was usually one his favorites of the entire church calendar. He explained to me, "I had decided this was going to be my year off. In 2017, I had gone into Lent with high hopes. Instead of giving up something, I would add something to my life: regular church attendance." Jon muttered something about that seeming like it might produce a similar amount of suffering, and then he continued: "I genuinely hoped that I would reestablish a spiritual home. But on Easter Sunday, I woke up and realized I had gone to church only once—on Ash Wednesday. So this year, I figured, 'Why even bother?'"

That all changed for Jon in an Atlanta gay club.

The weekend after Ash Wednesday, Jon flew to Atlanta to visit a guy he had met a few weeks before. They were on a clear path to dating. He had spent those weeks telling me about doing cute things like going to see the same movie at the same time in their respective cities, then buying the same bottle of wine and calling each other to compare notes. "I landed on the earliest flight, and we kissed the moment we saw each other."

Jon soon discovered, however, that this man had been hooking up with other people regularly, even after they'd had a long conversation around expectations, during which Jon had said he would be hurt if this guy was involved with other people. The weekend devolved from there. Jon told me later, "I was stuck in Atlanta with a man who was getting colder by the minute, trying to make the best of it because I didn't want to spend the money on an early flight home."

"We ended up in Midtown, hopping among clubs, a fake smile plastered on my face as I watched him flirt with everyone around me." Jon was awash in shame, in an unfamiliar city. Now, in addition to his shame, he felt anger. "I was angry at the shame and insecurity I was feeling. And at this dude who seemed to be completely free from all that—free enough to throw me aside and move on to the next guy."

I sat in my therapy chair, imagining the flashing lights and the vibrations of the deep bass as Jon continued. "I watched as everyone danced," he said, "seeming so joyful and free around me. And I decided I was done with it. I, too, could be shame-free, flirty, and fun, and I was going to prove it. Right after I finished crying."

Jon sent an SOS text to a friend from college, who mercifully showed up at the club to take care of him, but by the time the friend got there, Jon had decided that he *would* practice Lent. He was going to give up his shame and his insecurity. He told me, proud of himself, "I'm going to go to clubs every single weekend leading up to Easter, no matter what. I'm going to get over my fears. I'm going to flirt, go home with whomever, and do it all confidently. If the guy I almost dated can do it, I can do it, too."

AVOIDING SHAME

Shamelessness as a coping mechanism hides easily behind the label of sex positivity. In fact, sex positivity can become the banner cry of shamelessness. Anything goes and everything goes! "I'm going to have sex whenever and with whomever I want." But while shamelessness certainly functions within and contributes to hookup culture, I want to be clear up front that the kind of shamelessness I'm describing here has to do more with *why* we're having sex than with the actual sex.

I'm not here to draw lines around what is and what isn't healthy sex; that's for you to decide. I believe there's room within a healthy sexual ethic for hookups if that choice matches your values and desires. Shamelessness becomes an unhealthy coping mechanism when we throw all (or most) of our values away *as a way to avoid feeling shame*.

Often, we mistake the rigid boxes we tried to fit ourselves in for all aspects of our sexual selves. When we throw out the boxes that don't fit us, we may also discard some of our core values, too. We expect to feel free and liberated, but we may feel lost instead.

In the previous chapter, I discussed how we avoid shame through shamefulness, by hiding or attempting to control our sexuality. In contrast, when we use the *shamelessness* coping mechanism, we abandon all attempts at hiding, and instead, we bare ourselves to the world, loudly and proudly, declaring that anyone who doesn't like us now doesn't matter. Or maybe we decide to push down every single warning sign and red flag that pops up in our new shameless lives and deal with the consequences later. Instead of hiding from our shame, we stare it in the eyes and say, "I'm simply not going to feel you anymore." We push shame aside or into a corner within ourselves, and then we proceed with our fun.

And it seems to work, at least for a while.

For those of us who grew up in faith communities, the adoption of a shamelessness coping mechanism usually is accompanied by a faith deconstruction. The boxes we tried to fit in are part of larger systems of belief and values that no longer seem to work for us. We may encounter others who grew up in faith communities resembling our own and begin to notice patterns and similarities. As those systems become more and more transparent, we realize that the faith we were given in our childhoods is one we can no longer identify with or follow. If following God means living in those rigid boxes of regulation and shame, we would much rather leave our faith behind, too. And we have good reason to do so.

Anytime we try to get rid of our shame by just avoiding it, we run into problems. In the previous coping mechanism of shamefulness, we let shame control us by avoiding the reality that we are sexual beings who express our sexuality often and in many ways. That doesn't work because it's impossible to avoid our sexuality—it permeates almost every part of our being. When we cope through shamelessness however, we are trying to deal with shame by ignoring it. But shame doesn't disappear when ignored; it begins to seep.

One of the key indicators of seeping shame is a nagging gut feeling that something isn't quite right. We avoid dealing with that feeling head-on, for fear of what we'll find. When we're actively avoiding our shame, we fear that if we look too closely at ourselves and our actions, we will discover that we are terrible people.

Shame avoidance is similar to what happens when we stop paying attention to our budgets. If you're like me, you start spending money however you want, on whatever you want. It's fun. It feels good to spend the money. I always say something like "It'll work out," and I'll even glance at my bank account every so often to check the balance. But I can never entirely escape the fear that a bill is going to come up, and I'll discover to my horror that I went out to dinner too many times and now can't afford to pay rent. I never *actually* want to look at my budget. I never *actually* want to update it, because updating the budget makes it real. I have to face facts about how much money I'm spending on things I can't afford. Looking at the budget means the fun is over, and I'd so much rather feel that I have unlimited funds than realize that I need to cut back on the number of times I go to happy hour. But the fun of freely spending comes with a cost: the sinking feeling of dread that every time I put my debit card down, I'm a moment closer to a zero balance and not being able to afford the electricity bill. I can usually avoid that feeling of dread, but eventually, it catches up to me, and I have to reckon with reality. We can only avoid our shame for so long before we have to face it.

BLAMING AND DEFENSIVENESS

Looking directly at our shame is incredibly painful, so the tools of this coping mechanism—blaming and defensiveness—seek to keep the shame at arm's length. We react when anyone or anything gets too close to the shame that we're trying to keep pushed down. We get angry, we insist that we have the right to live the way we want, we struggle against any restrictions that resemble those that we've left behind. We blame those systems for the shame that kept us boxed in for so long and try endlessly to show how liberated we are, how shame-free we are. Anyone who doesn't believe us or cautions us to try another path gets blamed as well, and we cut them out. Because we're seeking to protect ourselves from feeling the shame that's lurking directly below the surface, we sit in a place of reactivity. Any time the shame feels close to coming to the surface, we pull out these tools. We're not the ones who are wrong, we're not the ones who have shame in our lives, *they* are. Everyone else is consumed by shame, not us. We're shame-free, obviously.

When we're out and about, hooking up with whomever we want, it can also feel shaming to actually admit that's what we're doing. That would mean looking at our shame head-on. If one of our friends gives us side eye for what we're doing, we're often quick to defend ourselves by blaming our actions on someone or something else. Like alcohol. Not everyone uses alcohol as part of hookup culture, but it's an incredibly common way of suppressing our fears and shyness, making it easier to connect with new people. So one of the most common statements for those coping with shamelessness is "I didn't mean to go home with him; I was drunk." All of a sudden, it's not our fault. It's the alcohol. Have a sexual experience that we aren't actually very proud of? Blame it on the alcohol.

Alcohol and other substances allow us to excuse ourselves from responsibility. And while it's certainly not a requirement for substances to be used while in this coping mechanism, the two usually go hand in hand.

Donna Freitas, a researcher who has spent considerable time interviewing people about their sex lives, points out, "Saying that you were drunk when you did something—even if you were not—will often get you a pass." She continues, "The shock of what someone did the night before—how far they went, who they were with, where they did whatever it was they did—can be lessened or even waved away if a person can say they were trashed at the time."[1] This is a pretty good test we can use on ourselves to know if we're in the midst of trying to cope with our shame or operating out of our values: Are we blaming what we have done on something else? If we're blaming, we're probably trying to avoid our own shame.

We may not actually believe that we're doing anything wrong while we're in this coping mechanism. And the truth is, we may be acting out of our values or working on developing those values while we're exploring shamelessness. Often, shamelessness can be a way station on the road to getting us to where we want to be. If we're having sex and using protection, we're taking steps to be healthy. But we haven't actually dealt with the shame that's under the surface. We are simply ignoring the shame and haven't worked with the wounds that are present.

A NATURAL REACTION

This coping mechanism is not unlike the period of natural development that teenagers undergo as they test their boundaries and explore their identities. And it makes all the sense in the world that those of us who were denied our adolescence by restrictive upbringings would need time to experience that period of exploration as adults. Instead of judging those parts of ourselves, let's recognize them for what they are: a natural progression—hiding, followed by a reaction to that hiding.

The point of naming the coping mechanism of shamelessness is not to add more shame to our lives, but instead to help us recognize and name the feelings within ourselves. Only after we've stopped avoiding our shame can we truly work through it. Our behaviors and actions may not actually change that much. But instead of acting from a place of defensiveness, instead of working to convince ourselves and everyone around us that we're free of shame, we're operating from a place of grounding.

When we're spending money that we've actually budgeted, we enjoy it more. What we're spending our money on may not change at all. We still go out at happy hour, but this time, when we put the card down, we know we're making a choice that works with the structures we've set for ourselves. That nagging feeling of "someday this is going to catch up with me" isn't present, because we know where we stand. We have nothing to worry about, because we are operating squarely out of our values, with intention.

How much better would our lives be if we could operate within our values and with intention in terms of our sexuality? What if the next time we have sex, we don't have to push the shame down, blame someone or something else, or feel like we need to defend ourselves against the people who remind us of the shame we're trying to avoid? When we're operating out of a place of grounding, the voices of people who don't agree with what we're doing are much less triggering. We know where we stand, so their voices don't actually reach us, and we don't need to respond.

FACING THE SHAME

"I feel like dirt. This isn't who I want to be." Several weeks after Jon decided to give up shame and insecurity, near the end of Lent, he was in a session with me, desperately trying to work with the anxiety and dread he was feeling. His shame was catching up to him, and he was crumbling. The night before, he had hooked up with a guy he had met at a club after they grabbed dinner and drinks.

"I had explicitly told myself before the date that I wouldn't go home with him. It's a weeknight, and I have stuff to do today." He shifted uncomfortably, "Yet somehow I ended up back at his apartment. The sex wasn't good, and after making some lousy excuses, I left his studio, feeling gross." Instead of feeling liberated, free from shame and insecurity, Jon felt everything he had been avoiding during Lent come crashing back. He felt sick. He told me he wanted to cast this guy aside, never talk to him again, and move on with his life. But the guy kept texting him, wanting to see him again.

Jon was caught between choices that all felt awful, which he explained to me with clarity: "I know I could ignore him and move on with my Lenten practice, or I can face the fact that I led him on. But that means I have to tell him that I don't actually want to see him again or have anything to do with him." Both felt like terrible options. Jon's values and actions were crashing against each other, and he was forced to stare his shame in the face. He not only felt shame for having hooked up at all—a remnant of the culture he had grown up in—but also felt shame for the way he had treated the guy. Instead of becoming a sexy, confident, liberated person, Jon said, "I feel like I'm becoming the guy who ditched me in Atlanta. I don't want to be that kind of person."

I reassured Jon that his feelings were understandable. He still had a choice. He could move back into alignment with his values, even though it meant some delicate conversations in the meantime.

The next week, Jon told me about the ensuing discussion he'd had with the person he had hooked up with. It was indeed difficult. "He was hurt and didn't understand why I was drawing such a strict boundary. I told him I don't actually want to see or talk to him again. He felt used." Jon felt that was true, but after that conversation, he began to feel realigned. By actually looking at his shame, naming it out loud, and taking steps to deal with it instead of avoiding it, Jon felt a wave of relief. He didn't exactly feel *good*—he had hurt someone—but he was back on track. Then we were able to start looking a little bit deeper at the sexual shame he was still carrying.

Notes

1. Donna Freitas, *The End of Sex: How Hookup Culture Is Leaving a Generation Unhappy, Sexually Unfulfilled, and Confused about Intimacy* (New York: Basic, 2013), 46.

CHAPTER 3.

AUTOPILOT

In the previous two coping mechanisms we've discussed, sex and sexuality are directed by shame. They happen in reaction to the shame that we're trying to avoid and/or control. But what if we've either worked through shamefulness and shamelessness or were never in those phases to begin with? What if we're pretty satisfied with our sexuality and our sex lives, and only feel shame once in a while? If this is the case for you, then when shame does pop up occasionally, you may not know what to do with it. This chapter is for you.

Sometimes, out of the blue, lying in bed after having sex with a significant other or after a hookup, shame pops up and makes us wonder if we're horrible people. We wonder if we're seriously messing up our lives by choosing to express our sexuality in one way or another, especially if we're expressing our sexuality in ways counter to our upbringing or the dictates of our faith community. The shame may feel relatively mild, or it may cause severe bouts of anxiety. Either way, eventually, most of us are able to shrug it off and move on with our lives—until it appears again.

If this sounds familiar to you, you're likely experiencing the autopilot coping mechanism. The underlying reality of this mechanism is that we're still not exactly sure what we really believe about sex and sexuality. We may have a rough idea of what our values are, but we haven't taken much time to define them. Without a clear definition for healthy sex and sexuality, shame can jump in and muck things up, causing us to question our actions and beliefs.

When we're operating on autopilot, we don't actually think much about our sexuality. We just take things as they come and rely on our instincts to get us through any difficult situations. In the first two coping mechanisms, we obsessively think about sex. In this coping mechanism, we're just living our lives until we find ourselves in a new or challenging sexual situation, and we're reminded, "Oh, yeah. That's something I was going to try to figure out."

Last year, I met up with my friend Ashley for brunch. She had just started seriously dating a new guy, and I was excited to hear how things were going. As I walked around the corner of the restaurant and spotted her in the window, I noticed she was looking more pensive than usual. "What's up?" I said as I greeted her and ordered coffee.

"Kyle and I had sex last night for the first time," she revealed, before our server was even finished pouring our drinks. Ashley always cuts to the chase. That's one of my favorite things about her.

I raised my eyebrows and slightly tilted my head. "And?"

She sighed. "I just don't know. I don't know how I feel about all of this. It felt good, but I don't know if *I* feel good."

Ashely was in the thick of the autopilot coping mechanism. Her shame manifested in the form of questions that are familiar to so many of us: Am I a bad person? Am I operating outside of my values? What *are* my values? Am I awful for not having values?

Just like most people living on autopilot, Ashley didn't have the answers to those questions readily at hand. We know a framework for our sexuality and sex lives would be helpful, but we don't know what that framework is. We don't want to go back to the other two coping mechanisms, but we don't have a clear alternative.

As Ashley and I talked, I realized that she hadn't gotten clear about what she actually believed about sex. She was caught in the middle between the restrictive sexual ethic she grew up with and a new sexual ethic that she hadn't fully formed yet.

If you're functioning on autopilot, you might feel a slight sense of dread anytime sex and sexuality come up. You're not hiding, you're not acting out, but you are aware that something still isn't quite right. Shame is lurking beneath the surface, and when it emerges, you don't know how to fight it. Overwhelming shame is less common for those who regularly employ this coping mechanism, but as with the other two, the sources and power of shame are still left unaddressed.

A CASE OF FUZZY VALUES

Quentin sat on a rooftop overlooking the waters of English Bay in Vancouver, British Columbia, watching the sunset with David, a guy he barely knew but with whom he felt safe. As they quietly sipped their wine, watching the pinks and blues play together on the water, he felt totally at ease.

There had been sexual tension between them for months, which they hadn't acknowledged, but now Quentin felt ready to make a move. "I just really want to kiss you," he said. David smiled, pulled Quentin in, and they kissed as the sunset transitioned to stars with the slight chill of a Pacific Northwest spring evening.

Quentin told me this story on a summer afternoon

when I was visiting Vancouver. We were walking the same beach he and David had overlooked a few months earlier.

"We jumped into his bed," Quentin continued, "and as we kept kissing, I told him I didn't want to have penetrative sex but was comfortable with us getting each other off. So that's what we did." Afterward, as Quentin reflected, he considered the evening a success. He had stayed true to his values in the moment and didn't go further than he wanted.

"I went home that night, because I had something going in the morning. When I woke up, I couldn't quite figure out what I was feeling. It wasn't shame. Or was it? Did I feel bad about doing what I had with him? Or did it feel great? Nothing seemed clear anymore." So, Quentin said, he shot David a text message: "How are you feeling?"

"Good," came the reply. "You?"

"Good."

He did feel good. Quentin told me, "I certainly didn't feel I had to repress a sense of shame, but I was a bit conflicted about what happened. I wasn't used to jumping into bed with a guy that quickly. But he seemed fine with it, so I shrugged it off."

Several days later, Quentin and David sat together in a coffee shop, trying to get work done. "I cleared my throat to get his attention and asked, 'Do we need to talk about what happened the other night?'" Quentin wanted to shine some clarity on what their evening had meant. "David looked at me, and I could tell immediately he wasn't going to say what I was hoping. He smiled and said, 'I really enjoyed myself and want to keep doing that with you, but I also know I don't want a relationship right now.'"

Quentin kind of did want a relationship but decided in the moment that the idea of spending time with David not just as a friendship, but physically, without putting labels on things, felt strangely comforting. "I decided to take him up on the offer of a casual relationship—friends with benefits."

They set frameworks for themselves, agreeing it would only work if they were able to be completely open in their communication. Quentin and David spent the summer hanging out, texting late at night, and ending up at each other's apartment often. "We were honoring our boundaries," Quentin told me, "but also exploring what it was like to have a relationship that neither of us had experienced before. It felt great."

Kind of.

"Usually, a day or two after we'd spent significant time together, shame would sneak up on me." Quentin looked down at the sand as we walked, sharing his shame voices with me: "Hey, remember how you're messing around with that guy? Doesn't that make you kind of slutty? Doesn't that make you a horrible person? You sure you still want to be calling yourself a Christian?"

"The thoughts filled me with anxiety," Quentin continued, "and I'd start questioning everything: Should I call things off? Should I try to move toward a romantic relationship with him to legitimize the fact that we were hooking up? Am I actually doing something I feel wrong about?"

"I couldn't put my finger on exactly what was happening, or how I really felt. Eventually, the shame would go away, I'd shrug it off and continue the relationship until the next time it popped up, and the next time. The negative feeling wasn't enough to change my behavior, but it was troubling, and I didn't know what to do about it."

Like Quentin, many of us are coping via autopilot. We settle here because it works. It's a pretty comfortable place. We're not debilitated by shame, and life feels pretty good. But we still have a sense that there should be something more. We might be sexually active, or maybe we've decided that we want to wait for some kind of commitment—whether that's marriage, exclusivity, or something else—before we have sex. Regardless, life generally feels like we have things figured out.

But, when we express our sexuality or have sex, we don't feel confident. We aren't operating from any kind of well-defined value system. Instead, we're making choices on the go, doing what feels good and right in the moment, trying to check in with ourselves, trying to live according to some fuzzy, poorly articulated values, and then evaluating the consequences later. Sometimes we're happy with our choices; sometimes we're not.

We may ask ourselves, as Ashley did, "Should I feel bad about this? Is it bad that I don't feel bad about this?" Or we may declare defensively, "I shouldn't feel bad about this. There's nothing wrong with my choices—but why do I feel like I'm making a mistake?"

If we have come from a faith tradition that teaches explicit rules around sexuality but have left some or all of that tradition behind, we might find ourselves struggling in this coping mechanism. Those rules provided a modicum of comfort and safety, because they told us what to do when things got complicated. Each time we faced a new or unknown situation, we could turn to the rules and usually get a clear answer very quickly. While those rules didn't always feel healthy or right, they offered a framework. We could evaluate our goodness or badness based on those rules. If we found that we were bad, they provided a way to become good. Just follow the easy steps. The path was narrow, but at least there was a clear path. However, many of us followed that path and discovered that it led to dead ends and shame instead of the land of milk and honey that was promised. At that point, all we had left was uncertainty.

A LACK OF CERTAINTY

The core challenge of the autopilot approach is a lack of certainty. We constantly ask, "How do I know?" How do I know which of my values are still being informed by the shame I grew up with? Have I thought deeply enough to know which values are truly mine? Are my actions informed by what I want, instead of something that actually works toward the well-being of others and myself? How do I know I'm not screwing things up? It can feel paralyzing, and often it feels easier to shrug off these questions and decide to deal with them later.

Anxiety, fed by shame and fear, is a manifestation of this coping mechanism. Sparked by this anxiety, we ask even more questions about ourselves: What if I'm wrong? What if I shouldn't be sexually active? Or what if I'm missing out by not being sexually active? What if I'm less of a person because of the choices I am making?

Sex always carries meaning. We want to do things right, care for ourselves and for others while engaging in a fulfilling sex life. The fact that our decisions around sex and sexuality usually have repercussions for others can add to the anxiety of this coping mechanism. It can feel weighty to have to consider our actions carefully as part of developing our own sense of ethics and determining the way we want to move through the world. For people of faith, the stakes feel even higher because we have deeply held beliefs, formed by God and Scripture, about the way we're supposed to exist in the world.

As Christians, Jews, Muslims, Hindus, and members of almost every other faith, we've been taught to love our neighbor as we love ourselves—a difficult yardstick to measure ourselves by. It makes sense that we turn toward rigid rules and strict frameworks, because they ease our fears. Rules based on Scripture and centuries of received wisdom help to assure us that we are indeed treating ourselves and others the "right way," and we don't have to be anxious if we just do as we're told.

So many of us have been harmed by shame-based teachings around sexual ethics, however, that we hesitate to adopt any rules or frameworks at all. We would much rather figure things out for ourselves, and that's how we find ourselves often engaging in unscripted improv scenes with ourselves and our partners, unsure of what we will say or do next. We find ourselves still wondering, "Is this the right way? Is there any right way?"

Instead of avoiding these questions, instead of avoiding our sexuality and sex lives, we need to dive deeper. As Ashley and I kept meeting up for brunch over the next few months, she started doing this. She spent time reflecting and began to articulate to me the values she did hold. She wanted to be close to Kyle and knew she wanted sex to be a part of building that connection. She let her questions be a guide forward as she explored and didn't let her past shame hold her back from trying new things.

It's important to realize that we can move past the autopilot coping mechanism and have a solid basis of values to stand on when shame strikes. To do that, we need to get to the root of our shame. The source of shame will look different for each of us. For some of us, it has to do with so-called biblical teachings around sex and sexuality —the rules our faith traditions have taught us about sex that make it difficult to expand our thinking and imagine healthy sexuality that is self-defined. Those lies include the idea that God and the Bible have a clear definition for healthy sexuality, and they span cultural and gender-based hierarchies.

In the chapters of part 2, I try to unpack some of the

lies that weigh us down as we try to formulate our own system of values and sexual ethics. The voices of shame are not from God. The voices telling us that we are terrible people, that we *should* feel guilty and awful about our sexual decisions, that we are always going to mess things up—those are the voice of lies. And it is to those lies that we now turn.

PART II.

LIES WE TELL ABOUT SEX
AND SHAME

CHAPTER 4.

"THE BIBLE IS CLEAR"

A few days ago, I was sitting with a client named Angela as she talked about how her desire to explore her sexuality was tempered by a fear that such exploration would put her ministry career at risk.

"There are people out there who would call into question my ability to be a pastor simply because I decided to have sex with somebody." Angela then told a story about a person she knew who had been a pastor for years. He also happened to be unmarried. He was forced to resign and leave his career behind because his church found out that he had a sex life. Angela was scared the same thing could happen to her.

And to be honest, I'm scared, too. If I had to boil down what I was taught about sex growing up to a single message, it would be "Don't have sex before marriage—no matter what." Abstinence before marriage was a litmus test, a way of figuring out whether someone was a true Christian or a pretender. Our sexual purity, I was taught, is one of the major things that separates us from "the world." On my bookshelf are books from when I was in high school that celebrate the rejection of premarital sex. In *Boom: A Guy's Guide to Growing Up*, the author devotes several chapters to clarifying the bright line between those who engage in sex outside marriage and those who don't. The benefits of waiting for marriage, as extolled by *Boom* and other books, pamphlets, and sermons like it, are numerous: no diseases, no unwanted pregnancies, no sexual baggage, no scars, no guilt, and ultimately "fun freedom" within marriage.[1] Yes, that's the term the authors of *Boom* used: fun freedom. Ultimate bliss. A sexual wonderland after saying "I do." Abstaining from sex before marriage would bring the promise of "a lifetime of guilt-free, comparison-free, disease-free, fully connected and committed sexual satisfaction."[2] Who doesn't want that?

I grew up believing these promises about the benefits of abstinence, and the truth is that some of them are true—at least somewhat. The only 100 percent effective way to avoid sexually transmitted infections is to refrain from having sex. And the only 100 percent effective way to prevent pregnancy is to refrain from intercourse involving vaginal penetration by a penis. (Queer folks definitely have an advantage on this front.) If only finding sexual fulfillment, avoiding a broken heart, and evading guilt were as easy.

Many of us still have a hard time overcoming the fear of sex instilled in us as children. In some ways, sex remains a confusing and terrifying prospect. If we don't wait to have exclusively monogamous sex within a committed, sanctified relationship, we think we will somehow be damaged. If we don't follow guidelines handed down by God (or so we're told), we will hurt other people and also will hurt ourselves.

My own parents often used 1 Corinthians 6:18 to drive home the importance of abstinence: "All other sins a person commits are outside the body, but whoever sins sexually, sins against their own body" (NIV). Even if it didn't feel painful, even if it felt good in the moment, sex outside of marriage was inherently damaging, they said. Even if

I didn't feel damaged, if I didn't feel guilty, if it felt like a solidly good experience, I would be tainted by any and all sexual activity before I met and married my wife.

As an adult and a professional devoted to helping people work through their fears and shame around sex and sexuality, I still worry about this notion of being tainted or damaged by sex. Is there something inescapable about sexual activity that will leave me deeply harmed, even if I'm unaware of it? There isn't a simple answer to that question, and the black-and-white approach our traditions offer us erases the complexity of sexuality. If we're going to work with our sexual shame in a serious way, we must work with the complexity, not try to avoid it with easy answers. We will look at some of the tools we can use to tackle that complexity in part 3. But first, we must examine the lies on which so many of our traditional approaches to sexuality are built.

TURNING TO THE BIBLE

When I was growing up, every time I asked an adult about the need for abstinence, they eventually answered simply, "Because the Bible says so." They would pull out a couple of key verses that warn against the danger of sexual sin and then would send me on my way. The problem is that when most churches define "sexual sin," they're making many assumptions about Scripture that deserve to be questioned.

Deconstructing our long-held beliefs can be scary and uncomfortable. Asking questions of the biblical text can be hard, but those of us who grew up believing that the Bible holds a prescriptive plan for human sexuality now have to wrestle and reckon with these texts if we want to overcome our shame, even if we don't turn to Scripture for guidance anymore. Regardless of where we are on our spiritual journey, if our bedrock sexual ethics are defined by the Bible and if we're wrestling with sexual shame, we need to examine those texts seriously. Our freedom from shame depends on it.

In the past, when I've asked probing questions about what the Bible really says about a topic—especially an issue as fraught as sex—I've been admonished by other Christians. "Don't be like the snake in the Garden," they'd say. "Don't ask, 'Did God really say?' Take it on faith that what our traditions say is true."

Those who believe the Bible is the literal and inerrant word of God regard any questions about the text as attempts to undermine their entire belief system. Pull at one thread, and you'll risk unraveling the whole tapestry. It's no wonder my Christian friends compared me to the snake in the garden of Eden—a symbol of temptation and evil—for asking a few questions. But maybe that tapestry needs to be unraveled. If a few questions can cause it to fall apart so easily, then maybe it wasn't very well constructed in the first place. As my friend Micah points out, we're asking questions "not to justify sin or to discredit God, but to find the *truth*."[3] And goodness, do we need a dose of truth when it comes to sexuality and sexual shame.

This story that my friend Charles emailed me will ring true for so many of us: "When I was fifteen or sixteen, my father bought me a book, *Every Young Man's Battle*, which promised to teach me how to 'remain pure in the real world of sexual temptation.' The cover of the book featured an image of a dude looking back at a blurry woman, similar to that 'distracted boyfriend' meme that was so popular in 2018. It didn't matter that she was blurry, because my eyes were only on him. I stared at him before reading about one of the author's dramatic attempts to suppress sexual thoughts about a woman he saw running on the side of the road. My immediate thought was, 'Well, not *every* young man's battle.'"

Charles's email continues, "The guy on the cover was hot, but I had a hard time relating to the stories in the book. 'Do other guys actually *think* these things about women?' With a bit of translation, and no help from the tiny five-page chapter tucked away at the end of the book called 'When Your Feelings Are for Other Guys,' I began to learn techniques for taking control of my 'thought life' in order to win the battle for purity."

Whether you're queer or straight or somewhere in between, if you grew up in an evangelical church setting, this quest to take control of yourself for the purpose of "purity" is probably uncomfortably familiar.

PURITY CULTURE

Purity is a vague term used by Christians of all stripes to restrict and control behavior, sexual and otherwise. It's fueled by Scripture passages like "How can a young man keep his way pure?" (Psalm 119:9) and "But among you there must not be even a hint of sexual immorality, or any kind of impurity" (Ephesians 5:30). That latter verse is what the authors of *Every Young Man's Battle* call the "single Bible verse that captures God's standard for sexual purity."[4]

Every Young Man's Battle is far from unique. So many books have been written to guide—or control—the sexuality of young people. Most of these books are geared toward women, not men, and were a driving force behind "purity culture"—a movement that emerged in evangelical Christian spaces most conspicuously in the 1990s. Purity culture focuses on a simple core message for young people: do not have sex before marriage. In many cases, the purity messaging prohibits any kind of touch or anything that might even spark arousal.

I'm part of the generation that spent our formative years mired in purity culture, and the deeply damaging effects of it are just beginning to be recognized. In her book *Pure: Inside the Evangelical Movement That Shamed a Generation of Young Women and How I Broke Free*, Linda Kay Klein points out that purity culture has left many of us "haunted by sexual and gender-based anxiety, fear, and physical experiences that sometimes mimic the symptoms of post-traumatic stress disorder (PTSD). Based on our nightmares, panic attacks, and paranoia, one might think that my childhood friends and I had been to war. And in fact, we had. We went to war with ourselves, our own bodies, and our own sexual natures, all under the strict commandment of the church."[5]

Klein writes that purity culture disproportionally affects women, teaching that women not only are responsible for managing their own sexuality, but also are required to monitor and regulate the sexuality of men. Purity culture tells women that, through the way they dress, the way they move, and the roles they play in churches and in households, they're the ones responsible for making sure the men around them won't "stumble" sexually. As a result, it cultivates an environment in which victim blaming and rape culture flourishes and results in debilitating shame for hundreds of thousands of women.

Let me be clear that I'm not attempting to speak for the women who have so profoundly experienced the impact of the purity movement. In the resources section at the back of this book is a list that highlights some of the many women who are leading the conversation about purity culture right now. We must listen to them and follow their leadership. For our purposes in discussing the lies that lead to sexual shame, however, it is enough to recognize that Scripture has been used in tremendously damaging ways to uphold purity culture, under the assumption that the Bible expresses one single and clear message about sexual ethics.

EXPLORING TRUTH

I want to directly challenge the assumption that there is one biblical message about sex and sexuality, but first, we have to take a step back and talk about what we mean when we say the Bible is "true." We may say that we're now living in a "post-truth" era, but truth is a concept that philosophers, theologians, and psychologists have been arguing about for millennia. What is truth? Does objective truth exist? Is it something that we can know? And when it comes to the Bible, the questions about what's true and what isn't only get messier.

One of the most often cited stories in the New Testament offers us some help in looking for truth. Just before his crucifixion, Jesus tells Pontius Pilate, the Roman provincial governor in Judea, that he came to "bear witness" to the truth (John 18:37). Pilate had the final say about Jesus's execution, and the text tells us that Pilate hoped to be able to spare Jesus's life but eventually acquiesced to the will of the crowd crying out for Jesus to be crucified. Pilate was torn. A question familiar to all of us haunted him: Am I doing the right thing here? Competing arguments swirled around; Pilate's gut was telling him one thing, the people close to him were telling him another, and the larger crowd was saying something else.

When I read this story, I imagine Pilate experiencing that deeply human feeling of insecurity and yearning for a clear direction. So when Jesus tells Pilate that he came to "bear witness" to the truth, it's no surprise that Pilate asks him an honest question arising out of exasperation or perhaps a genuine plea for clarity. It's a question that is all too familiar to anyone who has had to wrestle with seemingly impossible choices: "What is truth?"

Jesus stays silent.

His silence points us back to what Jesus first said: he came to bear witness. He doesn't give the Roman governor a clear answer, and he doesn't provide a philosophical argument about the nature of truth and morality. I think all of us would feel a little more comfortable if Jesus had told Pilate to grab a pen: "OK, Pilate, write this down, because I'm only going to say it once." Instead, Jesus's words ring in the air, intermingling with Pilate's question. *What is truth?*

Truth is something that is witnessed.

BEARING WITNESS

When we say something or someone bears witness, we're usually talking about results. For example, a few days ago, I went to a spin class. My heavy breathing and wet clothes afterward bore witness to the fact that I had gone spinning. The outward signs of exercise aren't the spin class itself; they are the result of it. If you had run into me as I was walking home, you would have been able to see the results of what I had just done, and you'd probably be able to figure out with some accuracy what the spin class was like, but you would still be a little bit removed from it. I bear witness, and you witness me. You're removed from the spin class itself, but you have connected in a small way to the experience of it through me.

Our human language is inadequate to describe the Divine, but metaphors do offer useful, though imperfect, windows into God's character. Jesus uses the verb *witness* as a helpful way of talking about the complex subject of divine truth. We know truth through witnessing it; it's not something that can be described in black-and-white categories. Like the sun, the light of God's truth is not something we can stare at directly. Instead, we know the nature of truth by experiencing it, by seeing the results of it. And that's precisely how truth works in our own tangible world, too. I can claim as much as I want that I'm telling the truth, but the experience of those who watch and listen to me inevitably will confirm or deny my claims.

When we hear people talk about the truth of the Bible's dictates regarding sex and sexuality, we must interrogate them, just as we do with any other scriptural claim. For example, Flat Earthers often cite scriptural references to the "ends of the earth" and declare that Scripture is clear about the earth being flat. However, all you need to do is look up photos of the earth from space, and you will quickly see that the earth is very, very round.

For many of us, it's so much easier to know what is *not* truth than what is. We can say confidently, "I'm not sure what truth is, but I know that's *not* it." The scientific method works in exactly the same way. We come up with some hypothesis of what could be true, and we test it through experience. Every time we fail, we get a little bit closer to truth, because we can say, "That wasn't it." When it comes to the ways we read Scripture and live out our lives as people of faith, as well as the ways we are transformed through that faith and become witness bearers, we can more easily look back and say, "Nope, not Truth," than we can say definitively, "I've arrived at Truth."

One way to look at our journey toward God and truth is that it is a process of becoming. I wonder if that's why the fruits of the Spirit that Paul talks about in Galatians 5 are things that can be experienced, rather than fact-checked: love, joy, peace, patience, kindness, goodness, faithfulness, gentleness, and self-control. Each of these things can be witnessed; they're the results of the work of truth and of God in our lives. We should be able to witness these things in our sexual lives, too.

This is not to say that we *only* come to truth through

experience. Nor is it to say that truth is individualistic or subject to personal whim. Obviously, at least within the Christian tradition, we believe that the Bible holds some authority in helping us arrive at truth, and we hold that belief with a great deal of seriousness. But we must be able to acknowledge when we get things wrong, especially when it comes to the ways that we read Scripture, including Scripture that deals with sex and sexuality. The lenses and the biases that we each bring to Scripture play a significant role in the way we understand the stories. Our personal, subjective lenses are inescapable, regardless of how often people in some branches of the church argue that they've arrived at "objectivity." Our lenses can cloud our vision or clarify it. In the same way we identify an incorrect eyeglasses prescription, experience is how we discover that our scriptural lenses need adjusting. Experience allows us to return to Scripture we interpreted in the past and say, "I thought this meant one thing, but it turns out to mean something else. Let's try this again."

We're human, we mess things up, we try our hardest to get things right, and sometimes we fail. We claim to be divinely guided but discover that we just *really, really, really* want to be correct. And, unfortunately, especially if we are in positions of power, we use Scripture deliberately to control others and impose our own agendas.

A SINGLE MEANING?

Let's return to the central question of this chapter: Do the Christian Scriptures teach rigid black-and-white rules around sex and sexuality? Does the Bible present one clear Truth on the matter?

The people who taught me about sex and sexuality when I was growing up would say, "Yes, absolutely. Scripture is all about black-and-white rules. All our teachings about sex and sexuality come directly from Scripture." But my response is to keep questioning and ask, "Where?"

The answer is more complicated than it seems at first. Sex is everywhere in the Bible. We don't have to be biblical scholars to look at the text and recognize that different kinds of sex are everywhere within the Bible: polyamory, sex with family members, sex outside of any form of commitment. Some Christians pay the most attention to lists of prohibitions—all the verses that say, "This is wrong." In those lists, we come across the word *fornication* often. Sometimes "sexual immorality" is substituted, but most often the word is fornication—a word that just sounds vulgar.

Here's where things get complicated. The Greek word that gets translated to fornication is *porneia*, which shares the same root as the word *pornography* in modern English. "Fornication" typically has a specific meaning in English today: sexual intimacy between unmarried people. Yet, in some churches, the meaning is subject to the whims of whoever is defining it, sometimes serving as a catchall for any kind of sexual activity they don't like—masturbation, for example. *Porneia*, similarly, has been used by people through the years to mean any number of forbidden sexual activities; yet its meaning is hotly contested and has been for a very long time.

Some scholars argue that *porneia* has a vast, complex meaning, encompassing any kind of sex that falls outside of a marriage covenant. These people acknowledge that when these verses were originally written, *porneia* may have had a more specific meaning related to cult-based sex workers. But they say church tradition has broadened that original meaning to include all kinds of "sexual immorality," with more and more being included in that definition every day. Other scholars argue that the meaning of *porneia* is actually pretty specific: temple- and cult-based sex work and incest. These people say that there's actually no indication that the definition of *porneia* should be broadened to mean premarital sex or any of the other sexual behaviors that often get thrown into the categories of sexual immorality or fornication.

The specifics of these arguments aren't crucial to our purposes here. If you're curious about these distinctions, by all means, type "porneia" into any academic search engine and get stuck in a research hole for days on end. As with most scriptural interpretation, you can choose your own adventure. What's important for our conversation is the realization that *porneia* is an ambiguous term with at least six different use cases in the New Testament, each meaning something different. For example, in Acts 15:20, the word appears to be referring to sexuality in idol worship; in 1 Corinthians 5:1, it seems to mean incest; and in 1 Corinthians 6, it seems to be referencing sex work. Yet each of these times, the word used in most English translations is "fornication" or "sexual immorality."

Most scholars agree that *porneia* is a word that wasn't very common at the time the New Testament books were being written in the first and second centuries, so we have to use context clues. Yet different scholars use different clues. If you wonder how individual Christian denominations can communicate such mixed messages about sexual ethics, one answer is that they're choosing among many different ways to interpret *porneia*.

Given the fact that *porneia* is hard to define, all sorts of people—scholars, theologians, pastors, random people in the faith club—are currently arguing about the meaning of *porneia*. The sides usually align with the larger value systems of those doing the arguing. Of course, it's problematic to think that each of us is just picking and choosing the interpretation we prefer, but I think there is something beautiful about the open space created by the ambiguous language of the Bible. It's almost as if the authors specifically chose words that had some breadth of meaning. It's almost as if the Bible wasn't written to be a list of moralistic rules and instead is a collection of books that bear witness to the indwelling of Truth in our world.

Since the meaning of *porneia* changes based on who's talking about it, we can see there is no single way of understanding what "sexual immorality" or "sexual morality" references in Scripture. And because we're ultimately seeking to assess the values we were given in childhood and perhaps develop a different set of sexual values, this is good news.

When we read that we must "flee from sexual immorality" (back to 1 Corinthians 6:18), we now see that "sexual immorality" is based on a term that theologians and ordinary people haven't been able to agree on for a good chunk of history. When faith leaders cite this verse and others like it to argue that the Bible teaches a particular, rigid set of rules around sexual ethics, and when they point to such verses and say, "See, it's right here; the Bible is clear," these leaders are not doing justice to the text or the truth.

Now when we ask, "Is this true? Is it true that the Bible is clear and unambiguous in defining sexual immorality?" we can arrive at a pretty clear response: "No. The Bible is broad and deep in its complexity and open to more than one interpretation of its meaning, especially around sexuality."

BEARING GOOD FRUIT

Given all we understand about the Bible's ambiguity, the passages about *porneia* are warning us about *something*. It's clear that Paul and the other New Testament writers take sex seriously and that they're calling us to take sex seriously as well.

As we have already discussed, we don't have to look far to see the risk for harm inherent in sex and sexuality, whether that be sexual shame from purity culture, LGBTQ people being named unclean, rape culture, or general everyday heartbreak. The list goes on and on. We also don't have to look far to see the deep goodness and beauty inherent in sex and sexuality. The Bible's authors do not shy away from acknowledging the profound impact sex can have.

Yet, while acknowledging that sex has impact, we also must be able to hold what we've been taught about sex and sexuality to the standard of bearing good fruit. For so many of us, the witness these teachings bear doesn't result in love, joy, peace, and all the other things Paul describes as good fruit. Instead, we've been left with separation, judgment, and shame. It seems that, for a wide variety of people, the normative "biblical" sexual ethic we've been handed by our tradition isn't working. We're at the cusp of something new, and we're seeing the harm that has been done. We see that our own experiences don't bear witness to truth, and the positive fruits of following abstinence or purity culture just aren't there. Now what?

We've spent some time exploring the supposed source of common Christian teachings about sex and sexuality, but we need to dig a little deeper. In the next chapter, we will turn to another lie that often gets misplaced in Scripture but has much more to do with Western culture and the development of the restrictive sexual ethic many of our churches bought into for centuries.

Notes

1. Michael Ross, ed., *Boom: A Guy's Guide to Growing Up* (Wheaton, IL: Tyndale, 2003), 85.

2. Ross, *Boom*, 85.

3. Micah J. Murray, "Hath God Said?," blog on Micah J. Murray's official website, August 29, 2013, https://micahjmurray.com/hath-god-said/.

4. Stephen Arterburn, Fred Stoeker, and Mike Yorkey, *Every Young Man's Battle: Strategies for Victory in the Real World of Sexual Temptation* (Colorado Springs, CO: WaterBrook, 2002), 3.

5. Linda Kay Klein, *Pure: Inside the Evangelical Movement That Shamed a Generation of Young Women and How I Broke Free* (New York: Touchstone, 2018), 8.

CHAPTER 5.

"GOD INVENTED PATRIARCHY"

As a young boy, I had a simple understanding of the relationships and spheres of women and men: I knew that the men around me seemed to fear and avoid women, except in specific circumstances. Because of that, I learned that women held a lot of power. The men in my church were always joking about having to check in with the "ol' ball and chain," suggesting that their own happiness hinged upon how happy their mothers or wives were at any given moment. Simultaneously, I discovered that any woman's power and autonomy could be snatched away with a firm word from a man. It was all fun and (demeaning) jokes until a man didn't get what he wanted; then the woman in question was required to submit.

These power relationships, I was taught, were based on the Bible, and the men around me had the verses to prove it. All the men in my community seemed to be both terrified and transfixed by the women around us, which often determined the way they expressed their sexuality.

In adolescence, my straight friends started to show a strange fascination with women and girls. What had once been scary and taboo became arousing. I watched as the guys around me began to realize that there was something about women they really liked—a lot of things, in fact. I also watched as many of my friends began to resent their new feelings and the young women who inspired them. Suddenly, guys' bodies reacted to these beings they had previously been told to avoid, to fear, to call "gross," or to exert dominance over "like boys do." An uncomfortable cognitive dissonance emerged, in which these guys were both desperately attracted to and fearful of the same young women. They both loved and hated their new relationships with women. And it soon became clear that most of the older men around me had never quite gotten over their resentment of women's apparent power over their feelings, even after they got married.

Many of us grew up in communities where women were tolerated, preyed upon, talked and joked about, fetishized, pitied, and silenced. The involuntary reactions men felt in their bodies were exaggerated to excuse other kinds of "involuntary" actions, such as rape. The reasoning went something like this: if arousal is involuntary, the actions that flow from arousal must be involuntary, or uncontrollable, as well. At the very least, it's all someone else's fault—*her* fault. Thus, women were blamed for men's actions, furthering both fear and fascination. I believe this complex and difficult situation for young men and women was the result of deeply held but ultimately false beliefs about biblical manhood, biblical womanhood, and biblical sexuality.

GENDER HIERARCHY

The norms of sexual expression in our society are rooted in the fear, oppression, and control of women, otherwise known as gender hierarchy or patriarchy. Women have been oppressed and controlled by men in many cultures for thousands of years. Societies were built on this false principle as far back as the second millennium BCE.[1] Some biblical scholars argue that this hierarchy is God-ordained, biological, and illustrated by the obvious physical differences between men and women. Those with this viewpoint say things like "Men are clearly designed to provide, and women to tend." These ideas are deeply rooted in our society's psyche and structures, but they are just a set of lies we call patriarchy.

Our own modern American culture (and most of Western civilization) is also built on patriarchy, and our common readings of Scripture hinge on this lie in ways that we are only beginning to understand.

We cannot have a conversation about sex and sexuality without acknowledging the lie of patriarchy and the ways it shapes so much in our lives, from religion to politics. In her book *Moral Combat: How Sex Divided American Christians and Fractured American Politics*, R. Marie Griffith outlines how views of gender roles are responsible for much of the conflict in our political systems. The division between "liberal" and "traditional" values often can be boiled down to views on gender.

As a gay cisgender man,[2] I am aware of the irony of my writing about the topic of patriarchy. It is absolutely essential for me to acknowledge patriarchy in this book, but because of my personal context and identity, I will do this inadequately. So let's be as clear as we can about the unclear territory we're in. In this chapter, I won't try to define and prescribe, but instead will describe what I've witnessed as a man swimming in the murky, pervasive waters of patriarchy and listening to the women swimming bravely against the currents around me. I hope I have listened and observed well and that I can point us all toward the work of the women who are reclaiming their stories and their bodies. Ultimately, we all need to be looking toward feminist, womanist, and *mujerista* leaders as they show us the way forward against patriarchy.[3]

LEARNING TO FIGHT

My friend Luke tells a story of his dad trying to teach him how to fight when he was little. His father showed him how to put his arms up to protect his face. As Luke focused intently on making sure his dad couldn't get a jab toward his face, his dad would go for his gut, and Luke would fall over, laughing, "That's not fair!"

Luke didn't particularly enjoy this play-fighting with his dad, and he told his father that he didn't need to learn how to fight because he didn't intend to fight anyone. Luke was pretty convinced, even as a kid, that he would never be faced with a need to defend himself physically. He protested, "I can talk my way out of it!" (He now tells me he has—every time.)

His dad let up but then said, "You're going to need to learn this someday, if not for yourself, then to protect your wife."

The message was clear: even if Luke never needed to defend himself, he would definitely need to know how to fight, just in case anyone ever threatened his future wife or girlfriend. His father explained, "That's because women are weak and men are God-ordained protectors."

While Luke was learning how to fight, my friend Rachel was learning how to dress. She remembers hearing conversation after conversation about being "modest." Modesty was the ultimate concern determining what she and her sisters wore, and it came up almost every time they went into a store. They had to be very sure that they weren't "causing their brothers to stumble." The modesty message was just as clear for them as the fighting message was for Luke, but no less frustrating: men are weak when it comes to their sexual drives, so it is up to women to protect them. Women's job of safeguarding everyone's virtue was considered God-ordained as well.

These stories were familiar to me and reminded me

of my own childhood. Thinking about all the ideas and ideals I had absorbed as a child and adolescent, I decided to explore more deeply what other friends and acquaintances had learned. I sat down with a small group and posed the question: What is the biggest lie you were told about sex and sexuality as a kid?

"That my sexuality is dangerous," my friend Jennifer responded, as she sipped a frothy cocktail.

It was a Saturday afternoon in March, a particularly beautiful time of year in Seattle, and we were overlooking the sunlit waters of Puget Sound as we talked. Jennifer is finishing up her PhD in theology and ethics, and her work focuses on reframing feminist theology in light of recent women's movements.

Jennifer continued, "Women have been told that men don't really have any control over their desires and that keeping ourselves safe and them safe means knowing how to hold our sexuality back or negating it altogether." It sounded very close to what my sisters had been told.

"Yes! Yes, yes, yes." My friend Kj was nodding her head vigorously.

Kj has a PhD in theology, imagination, and the arts and focused her research on feminist theology, literature, and pop culture. She is also my boss. "I was taught implicitly that I had no say over my sexuality, and it was up to other people—mostly men—to tell me what sex is for. The message was that women and girls could only discover sexuality in the context of being pursued by a man. Any sexual feelings of your own could only be expressed in marriage, with the approval and guidance of your husband. The idea that females might actually desire sex for pleasure was nowhere to be found."

At this point, my friend Alex was nodding his head, too. Alex holds a master's degree in theology and culture, and I graduated with him. Alex started describing his first "real" sustained romantic relationship, which happened in his early twenties. "I know this sounds so strange, but it really threw me for a loop when I realized that she actually wanted me as much as I wanted her. I hadn't been taught how to respond to a woman having desire."

I heard several loud groans in agreement, and everyone started talking at once. I recalled having been told by a professor that in Western psychology, women weren't even widely acknowledged to *have* sexual desire until the last fifty years or so. This realization probably could have been made earlier if any of the men doing the research had thought to ask (or listen to) women themselves.

Jennifer put it this way: "We've been told and have believed for so long that men are producers of knowledge and that women are consumers of knowledge. Women haven't been able to share their experiences, or when they have shared, they've been told it's invalid. This is a double whammy, because when women are told their sexuality isn't valid, they internalize that conclusion and begin doubting whether their experiences are authentic."

Later that same evening, I went to a birthday party for my friend Lauren. The party was at a massive German alehouse, the kind that serves beer in elaborate steins. The Seattle Sounders were playing against Vancouver, and it seemed like every soccer fan in the Pacific Northwest had converged upon the bar to watch the game.

I sat next to Lauren, and we tried to have a conversation, yelling over the noise of the soccer game and continually being interrupted by loud cheers. Lauren is finishing up her PhD in Christian social ethics with a concentration in women's and gender studies. I'm particularly interested in her work because she's researching how women and LGBTQ folk develop moral agency under the constraints of evangelical purity culture. Lauren had just written a paper about female desire and was sharing some of her findings with me.

She asked me, "Have you heard the phrase, 'Close your eyes and think of England'?" I hadn't. "It's sex advice women were given back in the Victorian Era, with the assumption that women wouldn't actually enjoy sexual experiences. They were told to shut their eyes tight and think of something pleasant, like England."

I shook my head. "Oh, my."

Lauren is also researching early church literature about female masturbation. She explained to me that we've been taught that women throughout the ages, but especially in the Victorian Era through the early twentieth century, were nonsexual beings. I nodded my head, remembering messages I heard in youth groups and from pulpits that were their own versions of "Close your eyes and think of England." Even today, many faith communities believe that sex is something for women to endure, not enjoy—an obligation for procreation.

"But," Lauren said, "I've been going back through and reading about letters sent between lovers—especially during wartime, when couples had to survive painful, long separations—and they're *incredibly* sexual. It seems that churches have been projecting a cultural ideal of what they want to be true of those women back onto history. Maybe a lot of women were having to endure sex, but there were also a lot of women who wanted and enjoyed sex as well."

What I've learned from conversations like these is that our religious traditions have taught us that sexuality has to look a certain way. This is rooted not in Scripture, but in a belief that gender hierarchies have to fit a particular structure, a belief that deeply damages every single one of us.

CONSTRICTED BY TRADITION

We're only beginning to deconstruct the ways gender hierarchy influences and constrains us, both personally and globally. The lie of patriarchy undergirds all of the messages we've absorbed about what sexuality must look like, and it creates a severely limited view of both sex and sexuality that is unsustainable.

Sexuality must be expressed only as heterosexuality.

Sex must be procreative.

The man must initiate sex, and the woman must oblige.

Sex must happen only within marriage.

It must, it must, it must—the "musts" have imprisoned us in countless ways, as we've refused to see the diversity, breadth, and depth of our innate sexuality.

Or our lack of sexuality. There are people in our world who do not experience sexual attraction, and I feel it's important to acknowledge this as well. Experiences of sexual attraction and romantic attraction are not universally experienced, and our asexual and aromantic siblings are often condemned for this. My friend Alejandra is one of those people. I posed the same question to her: "What is the biggest lie you were told about sex and sexuality as a kid?"

"That everybody is straight," she replied. We were in a coffee shop, and Alejandra stared over my head, remembering. "Once I began to realize my desires weren't for men, everything I had been told about sex and sexuality started to break down for me. And then I realized that sex drives are different from attraction, and that attraction is different from being romantic. I don't actually think I have those kinds of desires."

Alejandra identifies as queer, romantically attracted toward women, but on the asexual spectrum, meaning she doesn't experience sexual attraction. "I don't feel a strong desire for a relationship and definitely don't want to have sex. That seems to weird a lot of people out."

"Some people insist that asexuality only exists because of trauma," she added. "They'll ask invasive questions about whether I was abused as a kid and seem to believe that if I go to enough therapy, if I do enough work, then my issue will be resolved and suddenly I'll start experiencing sexual and romantic desire, like they do. We're told there's something wrong with us and that we need to be fixed."

Clearly, the diversity present within humanity is broader and deeper than many even imagine, and patriarchy seems to have impacted every bit.

LEARNING TO LISTEN

In our faith communities, women's voices have historically been missing from our discussions of sexuality—and in many ways continue to be silenced. Instead, sexuality has been framed, culturally, morally, and historically, to favor a very particular view of sex—a view that places men hierarchically over women and favors male expressions of sexuality.

In her book *The Birth of Pleasure*, ethicist and psychologist Carol Gilligan poignantly outlines a process that begins in early adolescence when young women start to realize that to fit comfortably and safely in society, they must silence their voices: "In adolescence, girls often discover or fear that if they give voice to vital parts of themselves, their pleasure and their knowledge, they will endanger their connections with others and with the world at large."[4]

Gilligan argues that this happens to men, too, but instead of learning to suppress their voices, they learn how to suppress tenderness and care. "Masculinity often implies a willingness on the part of boys to stand alone and forego relationships, whereas femininity connotes a girl's willingness to compromise herself for the sake of relationship."[5]

Every single person I've spoken with in researching this topic has reinforced Gilligan's point when, at some point in our conversation, they have said, "Patriarchy hurts men, too."

My message as it relates to sexuality and shame is that patriarchy harms us deeply in, among others, the ways it seeks to dictate what is acceptable and unacceptable regarding sexuality. For anyone who falls outside what is considered acceptable, this causes incredible amounts of shame. We may think, "There's something wrong with me," and only years later realize that the desires we hold, or don't hold, are God-given, and what is *actually* wrong is something deeply embedded within our culture. We need to find ways to heal.

I will end this chapter by deferring to the many women who are writing, speaking, and dedicating their lives to the work of dismantling the lie of patriarchy—allowing them to speak to the specifics of how we go about healing. There's a list of their works in the resources section at the end of the book. Each of us must learn to listen to those who have been told they must lose their voice to survive in our world. It's not a matter of "giving them their voice back," because they're already speaking. It's our job to search those voices out, see those voices as valid, tell them they're important, and then listen, and listen, and listen.

Notes

1. A fascinating exploration of this is Gerda Lerner, *The Creation of Patriarchy* (New York: Oxford, 1986).

2. "Cisgender" means I identify with the gender I was assigned at birth, as opposed to being transgender.

3. Womanist and *mujerista* approaches to theology and gender hierarchy sprang up as responses to white-dominated feminism. Womanism is primarily led by black women, and the *mujerista* movement is primarily led by Latinx women.

4. Carol Gilligan, *The Birth of Pleasure: A New Map of Love* (New York: Vintage, 2003), 29.

5. Gilligan, *The Birth of Pleasure*, 30.

CHAPTER 6.

"QUEERNESS IS SINFUL"

When I was fifteen, I came out to my parents. They immediately began researching ways to help me and quickly found resources from organizations called Exodus International and Focus on the Family, which promised that I would be able to change my "same-sex attractions" with enough willpower, prayer, and instruction. And then my education began.

One of the first things I learned was not to identify myself as my sexual orientation. I was not "gay." I was "same-sex attracted" or "SSA." I learned to keep this attraction mostly a secret, but when I had to talk about it, I would frame my sexuality as a struggle, telling a friend that I "struggled with homosexuality." If I were to identify myself using a word like *gay*, then, according to the program I was following, I was giving myself over to my sin and preventing the work of Christ in my life.

I lived like this for years, trying to bargain with God to change me so I would no longer be drawn toward the guys around me. I wanted to be "normal." I tried to dream of marrying a girl, of someday having a family. I believed that this was God's will for my life because my church and family had taught me that it was God's will for *every* young man: Grow up. Go to college. Meet a girl. Get married. Have a family.

When I was bargaining with God, I cut my sexuality off, consciously suppressing all desire. Every seemingly effeminate tendency I saw in myself, I attempted to change, paying close attention to the way I walked, the way I talked, and the way I used my hands when I spoke. Slowly, this suppression began to take a toll on my emotional life, as I was constantly crafting a false self that lived behind a broad smile and quick laughter. I was turning away, hiding because of all the shame I felt.

Eventually, noticing that my attractions weren't changing despite constant prayer, I gave up all hope of being in a relationship. I didn't feel it would be fair to lead any woman on, knowing that I wasn't attracted to her, but a relationship with a man was still out of the question. I resigned myself to being single, taking to heart the apostle Paul's assurance that the celibate life was a more holy life anyway.

FREEDOM IN CHRIST?

I was taken in by the lie—which is all too common in many of our church communities—that queerness is sinful. This lie encompasses so much, from the belief that it is a sin to identify as lesbian, gay, bisexual, or queer (or any of the other labels we now use to describe our sexual orientations) to the belief that identifying as any of the letters is OK as long as you don't *act* on those feelings. This lie focuses almost exclusively on sex, although debates around marriage can get wrapped up in it as well.

People who are advocates for the lie that queerness is sinful—along with advocates for patriarchy—argue that sex between men and women is part of the natural order of the universe and anything outside of that is a fundamental perversion of God's order. We can either choose to live according to what is natural and godly, which will lead to flourishing and fulfillment, or choose something else, which will lead to destruction and emptiness.

The faith communities I was a part of reiterated all the arguments, explaining that God "clearly" designed men and women to "go together," and any deviance from this was against God and, using the language of Leviticus, an abomination. Not only would I be subject to the fires of hell if I were to follow my sinful desires, but I would also reap the consequences within my own body. This teaching led me to fear my sexuality and my body, pushing me further and further into isolation.

Proponents of the lie about queerness suggest that there are specific environments, such as straight marriages, in which humans fundamentally flourish and other environments, like queer marriages, that lead to destruction. This teaching is common in Christian theology. But when I look back at the ten years I spent suppressing and hiding my sexuality, I can't help but wonder what flourishing is supposed to look like in this context. I followed the advice of my parents, pastors, and theologians by centering my life on everything they told me was pleasing to God. The resulting shame, isolation, fear, and psychological dis-integration didn't feel like flourishing in any sense of the word, despite all assurances from my Christian friends that I was following a difficult but godly path.

Regardless of how I felt, regardless of the adverse effects of this anti-gay, anti-queer theology on my life, I was allegedly free. I believed that to turn away from these teachings and pursue a life that felt more freeing, more integrated, and healthier was to buy into worldly deception and chains. In other words, according to my spiritual mentors, what felt like chains at the time was actually freedom, and what felt like freedom was actually chains.

A paradox exists in the teachings I was trying so hard to believe and live by. Freedom in Christ may not feel like freedom, those lessons implied. In fact, it can feel exactly the opposite.

"YOUR CROSS TO BEAR"

"I'm sorry this is so hard for you, but it's just your cross to bear. We each have our own crosses in life."

I've often been told something like this, ostensibly to ease my burden. Many believe that the Christian life isn't easy and that suffering is to be expected. Each person has certain struggles, or "crosses," to bear, and those can help us feel closer to Jesus. My mother, for example, taught me that none of us get through life without certain sins that plague us. She told me that her cross was pride. For others, it could be alcoholism, lying, worrying, or lust. Mine appeared to be homosexuality. The key was not to over-identify with these struggles, but instead to hand them over to Christ and let the struggles shape us into the likeness of Jesus.

Biblical passages that equate suffering and hardship to future glory are common, including the apostle Paul's "thorn in the flesh" (2 Corinthians 12:7) and his teaching in Romans 8, which proclaims, "Our present sufferings are not worth comparing with the glory that will be revealed in us" (v. 18). Christian theology suggests that following Jesus will inevitably result in suffering, and that will eventually lead to true freedom. We are taught to rejoice in our suffering, because it produces perseverance, character, and hope. It is what shapes us into the likeness of Jesus—the fire that produces the fruits of the Spirit.

Even now, I don't doubt these teachings. Some of the most beautiful experiences in my life were born in periods of struggle and pain. There are moments in life that feel like death, but the act of dying brings about abundant newness. This is the nature of the universe, reflected in the death and resurrection of Jesus on the cross.

The argument for some human suffering is simple: struggling with one's sexuality might feel like a form of torture or death, but it is nothing more than what Jesus calls every person to.

But some people take the call to suffering a step further, warning that even identifying as part of the LGBTQ community or as having a sexual orientation other than heterosexual is to implicitly reject the work of Jesus on the cross and step fully into sin, a state that is intolerable. People in my faith community told me the same thing, using Paul's list of sins in 1 Corinthians 6 to argue that by calling myself gay, I'm slapping God in the face and blaspheming against the work of Jesus on the cross. In some modern translations of the Bible, 1 Corinthians includes "homosexuality" in a list of sins.

"If we deliberately keep on sinning after we have received the knowledge of the truth," say some modern ministers, quoting Hebrews 10, "no sacrifice for sins is left." Proponents of this argument are making a grave, even deadly, error that reveals their blindness to their own sin. In fact, they are doing precisely the opposite of what they claim. They are denying that Jesus offers abundant life to what we might call sexual minorities, driving us away from faith communities, and binding us to darkness and death.

For people struggling with their sexuality, the "freedom" peddled by those who claim orthodoxy has consistently come with profoundly negative effects, including depression and suicidal ideation. Yet people who hold traditional views ignore this reality, arguing that any suffering we might experience now will matter very little when compared with the reward waiting in heaven for the one who chooses the narrow path. There is a certain stubbornness built into this mind-set: as long as you are following a traditional understanding of Scripture, it doesn't matter what the results are, even if they are deadly.

A NEW STORY

The idea that queer sex and queer relationships are inherently sinful comes from about six verses scattered throughout the Bible. I don't want to get into parsing those verses here, for two reasons: First, the meaning of these verses is even more hotly contested than the meaning of *porneia*, discussed in chapter 4. Second, plenty of books and essays are still being written about the mistranslations and misunderstandings of these six verses, and we don't have the space to do them justice here. The resources section at the end of this book lists sources of more information.

For our purposes, it is enough to point out that the traditional interpretations of these verses aren't the *only* interpretations that are faithful to the text. Furthermore, when we look at the fruit borne by traditional teachings about queerness in the lives of LGBTQ people, we can clearly and conclusively say, "This is not true." Just as we can learn from the witness of women as they share with the world the harmful results of restrictive and patriarchal sexual ethics, we can learn by listening to the witness of LGBTQ people as we share about the damage that non-affirming interpretations of Scripture have had on our lives.

But sometimes saying simply, "This is not true," isn't enough to banish shame without providing an alternative interpretation. We need a new narrative—and thankfully, we can find that narrative right within the Bible itself.

In the second creation myth found in Genesis, after God created the universe, God formed a person out of the dust of the earth. I like to picture how carefully God did this, spending time getting every detail right, meticulously crafting this person's nose, their eyes, imagining how each part will work, maybe chuckling a little bit while dreaming about all the silly antics they're going to get up to while living in the garden.

Once everything was perfect, God breathed into this *ha-'adam*, literally translated as "earth creature," and the creature came to life. Biblical scholar Phyllis Trible points out that while most of our Scripture translations today use he/him pronouns for this earth creature, in the original Hebrew the *ha-'adam* is undifferentiated.[1] It is not accurate to say that the "man" or Adam was created first, because Genesis doesn't begin distinguishing gender until later in the story. The first human was gender expansive, gender inclusive, genderless.

God planted a garden for this earth creature and began showing it off to them—the trees and the rivers, the precious stones, and the delicious food all around and available for them to eat. While God was showing off all this perfection, God's face fell. Something wasn't quite right. God looked at the earth creature and realized that they didn't have a companion. There was no one for this earth creature to be with, and God declared something "not good" for the first time.

You see, up until this point, God had looked around at everything she'd created and had given herself a little nod of approval.[2] "Yes, this is very good," she'd said after making the sun, the moon, water, and all the animals. I often laugh at this part of the story, because isn't this what we all do? Anytime we create something we're particularly proud of, exercising all our creative gifts, we usually take a step back and look at it, muttering something like, "Yeah, this is pretty amazing. I love this!" Up until this point in the Genesis narrative, God was simply reveling in her handiwork, excited to show it all off. But when God realized that the earth creature was alone, she changed her tune, declaring somewhat dramatically, I imagine, "This will not do. This is *not* good."

The story reveals a fundamental truth about humanity that science continues to confirm again and again: humans are wired for interaction, for companionship. As recent discoveries in neurobiology show us, and as therapists have been telling us for decades, we cannot survive without the presence and love of other human beings. Personhood cannot be formed without other persons. We are entirely dependent on communication with others for our brains to develop. As God realized at the dawn of creation, it is *not good* for humans to be alone.

In the next scene of the story, God took the earth creature and showed off all of the animals that she had created. The two turned it into a game, as God let the earth creature name each and every one of these animals. I imagine the both of them laughing and playing as God said, "Look at this one! And over there—how about that one?" At the same time, there was a little bit of a frantic search, a tiny feeling of discontent in the garden. Things still weren't right.

As animal after animal got a name, fewer and fewer remained to be considered for the role of the perfect companion for the earth creature. I imagine the earth creature, after giving the last animal a name, looked at God and asked, "That's it?" God slowly dropped her head and nodded, "Yes, that's it." The search for the right kind of companion to take away the earth creature's loneliness was over, and no one was suitable.

Some people hear this story and are quick to say, "Wait, but the human wasn't alone! God was beside them, and perhaps a dog, maybe a cat or two." For many of us, that's not aloneness; that's a recipe for a pretty fulfilling life.

Even so, as God and the earth creature walked away from a day of naming and searching, things in the garden still weren't right. The human was still alone, feeling a kind of aloneness not even God's presence could fill, let alone a dog or a cat. The earth creature needed *someone else*, in addition to God and other living beings. Things on earth weren't going to be good until this someone else was found.

We all know the rest of the story. God cast a sleepy spell on the earth creature and formed a woman out of the earth creature's side. It is when the earth creature wakes up that we see gender appear for the first time in the Bible: man and woman, Adam and Eve. In each of the creation stories found in Genesis, the genders are distinguished at the *exact same time.*

"At last!" Adam said, relieved, "There's someone like me! Bone of my bones, flesh of my flesh!" Notice, that after all this hubbub of naming and searching, the companion that the human needed was someone *similar*. As biblical scholar James Brownson says, it is not the *difference* between man and woman that is highlighted in this narrative, it is *similarity*.[3] The story goes to great lengths to show that the companion was good because the companion was the same as the earth creature.

SACRED SPECIFICITY

We see in the Genesis 2 creation story an essential truth about the nature of human relationships that some theologians call "sacred specificity." For humans to thrive and flourish, they need to be in particular relationships with particular other humans. This is a point that I think is often missed, but we see it reinforced again and again, throughout Scripture and in everyday life. Humans need to be in relationship to others, but not just *any* relationship will do. The earth creature needed a companion, so

God created Adam and Eve, together. The earth creature was transformed into Adam and Eve, particular humans created to be in relationship with each other.

This idea that not just any relationship will do for each of us is found throughout Scripture. There's something specific in the relationships between, say, Ruth and Naomi, David and Jonathan, Jesus and his disciples, or Christ and the church that allows each person to flourish in particular ways. We see this even in the way that the Christian concept of salvation is traditionally described. Not just any relationship will lead to salvation, but it is only a relationship with Jesus that allows us to step into new life.

The specificity of a particular relationship leads to the flourishing of those in the relationship, and this specificity is sacred. When we're looking for an intimate partner, someone to marry or enter into a sexual union with, not just anybody will do. It takes someone special, someone who seems to be "made just for us." Incredibly complex psychological, biological, physical, and spiritual processes are happening just underneath the surface when people come together and become something more through their relationship. This occurs not only in intimate relationships but also in friendships, in business partnerships, and in the collaborative creation of art, literature, and music. In each case, the particularity of each person is important to the creation of the something more.

CUTTING PERSONHOOD

As a result of the failure of every major ex-gay "ministry" attempting to change people's sexual orientation, many churches have now accepted that sexual orientation rarely, if ever, changes. But the guiding principle in many traditional churches is still to name all same-sex sexual and romantic activity as sinful. Many churches have adopted a "welcoming but not affirming" approach that requires queer people to take a vow of celibacy to stay within the good graces of church fellowship. This approach to queer people within church communities is wreaking havoc upon millions of lives.

Let's be clear-eyed about what's happening in the name of biblical "truth." By holding firm to misinterpretations of Scripture that declare homosexuality as sinful, forced celibacy is peddled to sexual minorities as being God's "best." This form of celibacy often leads queer people to the opposite of relational flourishing; it leads to isolation, depression, and suicide.

There is something deeply wrong in a theological approach to queer people that denies them the possibility of intimate relationships. By not attending to the sacred specificity of sexual orientation—the relational wiring of sexual minorities—people within the church are pushing countless queer people toward death instead of life. Denying anyone, not just sexual minorities, the possibility of intimate relationship cuts them off from the potential of relational flourishing in two ways.

First, since the particularity of sexuality is a core part of our beings, and since we cannot box off just a portion of ourselves without affecting the whole, removing even the potential of intimate relationship begins the process of removing someone from their self. Sexuality is tied to our ability to love. When a particular sexual orientation is labeled as "bad," that message is impossible to separate from an indictment of the person's entire self. To say that your sexuality is disordered is to say that your capacity to give and receive relationship is disordered. Thus, the process of depersonalization begins.

Instead of leaning into your true self—the reality of your sexuality—a false self is constructed, which can take several forms. The most extreme form of the false self is attempting to adopt an identity that is different from reality. This was the goal of "ex-gay" ministries. Your false self can also be constructed by attempting to quell any and all sexual feelings and desire for relationship. Instead of fostering a healthy and integrated sexuality, this is forced asexuality, which causes a mind-body split and often results in unhealthy ways of managing your sexual feelings. No one can operate in a false self without dire consequences.

Cutting ourselves off from any potential of intimate relationship also cuts off our ability to understand and communicate with ourselves, because any such attempt is labeled as "bad" or "sinful." In Christian households advocating this position to sexual-minority teenagers, the teenager has no choice but to operate out of a false self in any relationship. As philosophers and theologians point out, the moment a person begins suppressing their own truth and reality, true relationship ceases. Instead, a facsimile of relationship begins, with the queer person pretending to be someone they are not. The result is a fracture at the core of their personhood. We no longer are our true selves, but instead are a caricature of others' expectations. We aren't able to give love and have no outlet for our sexuality. The internalized message becomes, "I am not worthy of giving love." We can see clearly how shame is born here.

Second, cutting off our ability to give relationship also cuts us off from our ability to receive relationship. A precedent is established: "I must be something else to be loved." Instead of being celebrated and affirmed simply for being ourselves, the message explicitly and implicitly is, "I am not worthy of relationship unless I become something different." The roots of shame grow deeper and more complex here.

We see the results of this idea in much of queer culture today—changing and twisting and warping ourselves to be "worthy" of love and belonging. This is not a critique of queer culture, but instead a critique of the systems that have not allowed queer people to grow into healthy relationships. Instead of learning to rest in the outflowing of love and belonging that should be present in all relationships, we aren't able to receive and accept what is being offered. The internalized message becomes stronger: "I am not worthy of receiving love."

It's important to note that the lie of patriarchy is deeply intertwined with lies about queer sexuality. The two are connected because queer sexuality is a threat to hierarchical gender roles. Unfortunately, being queer doesn't eliminate the possibility that you will be a part of the problem. Gender hierarchy and patriarchal ideals thrive in queer culture, too, and often exist almost unchecked in gay male culture.

As an aside, I must point out that there's a difference between the prohibition of queer relationships and people *choosing* to be celibate for any number of reasons. Prohibition also differs from someone having difficulty finding a partner. Prohibitions are forced, whether through explicit doctrines or subtle cultural and spiritual cues. If we can all grow and develop in a space where our capacity and desire for relationships, intimate and otherwise, aren't called into question, and then *choose* to be single, that's a whole different story. Shame won't get a stronghold in that kind of scenario. However, the two cannot and must not be conflated. Arguments that highlight the rich traditions of celibacy within our faith communities or that use Paul's writings about celibacy as support for *mandated* celibacy based upon specific sexual orientations are severely misguided. Freely chosen celibacy may come from a place of health, while prohibition of sexual relationships on the grounds of who we are attracted to leads to spiritual, psychological, and even physical death.

POTENTIALITY

The above ideas can be summed up neatly: cutting off the possibility of intimate relationship removes our *potentiality*. Potentiality is a fundamental part of human nature, because as humans, we are continually becoming; we never arrive. We always have the potential to flourish, but not a guarantee. By eliminating the possibility of intimate relationships, our ability to become and develop is also removed.

As we have established, being cut off from intimate relationship affects every other relationship in our lives. The queer person, instead of learning how to flourish within all forms of relationships, is removed from those relationships entirely. Many of us inhabit a secret life within a false self. This type of existence thwarts opportunities for development and leaves us in isolation and loneliness. Instead of being drawn into community, we are excluded, attempting to simultaneously hide our sexuality while presenting a false self to the world.

We thus experience aloneness at its darkest. We are isolated, and isolation is inherently traumatizing and dangerous. For the isolated queer person, almost every moment is spent wondering how people will respond and whether we are passing as "straight enough." There is no room for growth in these spaces, no movement outward. Instead, a turning inward happens, and isolation often leads to depression, anxiety, and suicide.

In the creation story of Genesis, we find a truth that we can all bear witness to: it is not good for humans to be alone. The aloneness in this story can be banished only through intimate relationships with other humans. When institutions cut off our potential for intimate relationship, shame emerges and fills the void, with disastrous consequences.

If we were raised in an environment lacking intimate relationships yet manage to survive, undoing our shame takes years. We can fight shame only in the presence of community; we need other people to come around us, bearing witness as we speak the lies we learned about ourselves, lies that we have internalized at our very cores. As we speak those lies, our shame slowly loses its power.

The value of an affirming community cannot be understated as we work to re-narrate the lies we have been told about ourselves. Support can come in many forms, including online support groups, affirming faith communities, and friendships. A good therapist well versed in the combination of religious shame and the shame that comes from being a sexual minority can be a guide and companion in our healing.

In part 3 of this book, I offer a method for individuals and communities who are working to support each other and to deal with the shame that comes from lies about biblical teachings related to sex and LGBTQ identities.

Notes

1. Phyllis Trible, *God and the Rhetoric of Sexuality*, Overtures to Biblical Theology (Philadelphia: Fortress Press, 1978), 80.

2. As an active way to interrupt patriarchal constructions of God, I'm choosing to use female pronouns for God in this story.

3. James Brownson, *Bible, Gender, Sexuality: Reframing the Church's Debate on Same-Sex Relationships* (Grand Rapids: Eerdmans, 2013), 26.

PART III

MOVING BEYOND SHAME:
THE PARADOXES OF SEX

CHAPTER 7.

PARADOX 1: SEX IS HEALTHY AND RISKY

Now that we've explored how we often respond to sexual shame and looked at some of the lies we've been told about sex and sexuality, we can turn to this question: How do we begin to recover? I've talked to countless people who want to take sex seriously—not in a restrictive, grave way, but in a way that holds some intentionality. These conversations often boil down to one main point: I want to feel confident and free in the way I express my sexuality. Since sex is usually a relational act, we want to hold concern and care for the people in our lives that we choose to have sex with, and we want to do so in a way that feels ethical and life-giving to all who are involved.

The struggle is about how we can be intentional around sexual ethics without falling back into the same pit that purity culture put us in—a pit of rules and regulations and morality and shame. Is there a way to approach our sex lives that allows us to engage in a way that not only avoids moral prescriptions but also fights the very shame we're plagued with? I believe the best way to do that is to talk about what sex *is* instead of what sex *isn't*. For so long, we've been told everything about what sex is not, what sex shouldn't be. It's much less common to have conversations about what sex is.

So much of our sex lives is personal and particular, based on each of our own contexts, and this fact makes having a single, universal, one-size-fits-all sexual ethic impossible to arrive at. Still, I believe sexuality contains four paradoxes that, when acknowledged, help us chart a path forward in our conversation on ethics and simultaneously help us understand our shame and thereby get free of it. By understanding these paradoxes, we become more equipped to handle our shame and figure out what our core values are in the process. Once we know our core values, we have ground from which to evaluate our decisions. We can look at the choices we're making and ask, "Does this align with who I want to be?" Instead of using coping mechanisms to deal with our shame, we know our ground. We know where we stand.

And the beautiful thing about these paradoxes is that they allow for fluidity. As we continue to have new experiences—as we explore, as we enter relationships or exit marriages, or as we discover that we're attracted to different sorts of people than we thought—of course what we believe about sex and sexuality will change. Our framework and ways of thinking need to be able to adjust, and these paradoxes help with that. We'll explore the paradoxes in this chapter and the following three, starting with the first paradox: sex is healthy and risky.

SEX IS HEALTHY

There's no question about it: sex is healthy—and not just a little bit healthy. From increasing levels of antibodies that help fight sickness, to reducing depression, to making us look younger, sex has been shown in study after study to have profound effects on our physical and emotional well-being. We are sexual beings, and having sex (with a partner or on our own through masturbation) is good for us. Sex is both healthy and positive. A sex-positive sexual ethic, built on the idea that sex is healthy, is a powerful antidote to shame.

Of course, not all sex is good sex, not all sex is healthy, and not all sexual experiences are positive. But our sex-positive sexual ethic must begin with this premise: good and healthy sex is possible in any number of scenarios.

Those of us who were taught restrictive and shame-filled rules about sex may find even this basic definition hard to grasp. If you're feeling a bit uncomfortable just reading these words, try holding the premise as a question. What if sex is healthy? What if sex is a positive thing? If these assumptions are true, how might that change the ways you relate to your body and your sexuality? You don't have to accept my word for it; changing beliefs we have grown up with takes time. Simply asking the questions is enough of a start.

For others, this may seem like a no-brainer. Obviously, sex is good for us. We might not have any trouble exploring our bodies, enjoying our partners' bodies, and experiencing pleasure. We might know the goodness that having sex can bring, and it doesn't take any convincing for us to believe that sex has profoundly good and positive effects on our lives. If that's you, great! This chapter is for you, too.

Many of us grew up hearing that sex is dangerous. We saw graphic illustrations about what happens to us when we have sex and about how having sex would change us forever. We imagined ourselves as chewed-up pieces of gum, trampled roses, and mangled bits of paper. We were told sex has the potential to ruin our lives, mar us beyond recognition, make us undesirable to future partners, give us any number of STIs, and possibly cause us to wind up pregnant in the process. We're not going to say that here.

The truth is, sex is healthy, *and* it is risky. Acknowledging the inherent risks involved in sexual behavior doesn't diminish its positive nature; it is recognition of reality. Despite all the goodness that sex can bring us, like most things in life, it involves the potential for harm. And because sex carries the potential for such health, for such flourishing, it also contains all the elements to do the opposite of those things, too.

Due to residual trauma, and I'm not throwing that word around lightly, those of us who have come out of conservative and restrictive backgrounds will often react very strongly to anyone suggesting that sex might be dangerous. Our antennas go up when we hear language and messages similar to those we heard growing up. We bristle. And you may be feeling that bristly feeling as you read this. Don't push those feelings away. Pay attention to what comes up as I discuss the idea that sex is risky.

Note my choice of language. I imagine that we can all agree that sex can certainly be used in dangerous ways, as a means of exerting power and control. But, there's nothing about sex that is inherently dangerous. Some of our work to overcome shame will be learning how to undo the voice inside of us that tells us to stay away from sex, to keep our distance, to calm the warning alarms that go off any time we begin feeling arousal.

But, sex *is* risky. "Risky" simply means that it carries risk. The distinction here between dangerous and risky is crucial. Saying something is "dangerous" implies a certain level of certainty that it will lead to destruction or harm, but saying something is "risky" implies that we need to be careful. Danger may be in the picture, but it's not a sure thing.

I go hiking with a group of friends about once a month. Here in the Pacific Northwest, we are surrounded by trail systems that range from easy to risky to downright dangerous. While several people in the group are experienced hikers, I'm not one of them. I refuse to buy hiking boots on principle, because I would rather not be one of *those people*. You know the ones—they always carry Costco packs of snack bars in their North Face backpacks and are continually searching for their expensive eco-friendly water bottles, which they left at brunch *again*. "No, these Toms shoes are fine," I say, pulling on my favorite shoes that are more like slippers.

And for that exact reason, I only get invited on the hikes for new people—the easy hikes. Even on these reasonably simple hikes, we spend time before we begin double-checking our gear, making sure everyone has enough water, checking that we have enough food with us to survive for a bit in case something goes wrong. There's nothing particularly dangerous about most of the hikes, but we approach them with the understanding that they are risky. Any time we venture out, we understand that there's the potential that something could go wrong. Someone could get hurt, someone could get lost, we could run into bears or mountain lions—and we prepare accordingly.

Fortunately, nothing has gone wrong in all my years on the trail, but even routine and easy ventures out into the wild can turn into a survival situation at a moment's notice. This is because we are interacting with forces of nature that are so much bigger than our individual selves. Does this mean we shouldn't go hiking? Does this mean we should save hiking until we have a commitment from the trail that it's here for us through thick and through thin? No. But it does mean that we have to be aware of the risks, and by taking these risks seriously, we can enjoy our hikes much more.

Similarly, to truly have a grounded sexual ethic, we have to be aware of the risks inherent in sexual activity. Knowing these risks will help us prepare, anticipate, and choose how we will respond to these risks instead of living from a place of just reacting.

Neuroscientists and psychologists are only just beginning to understand the incredible forces within and around us that affect our sexuality and sex lives. An understanding of these forces and the ways they affect us for good and open us to potential for hurt, will help us decide how we want to navigate the complex terrain of sexuality.

SEX AND CONNECTION

Sex is both healthy and risky because sex connects us. This is an inescapable truth built into the very act of sex: physical connection. Even if we're in it just for the physicality, only to fulfill an urge, we're still connecting with another person. Purity culture has weaponized this truth to say that if we connect with someone sexually and then decide to move on from that person, we will be irreparably harmed. That's not true; having sex doesn't automatically mean harm is in our future, and even if harm occurs, we have tools to heal. But the fact remains that having sex is one of the most powerful ways we can connect with a person.

Helen Fisher, senior research fellow at the Kinsey Institute, denies that "casual" sex is really possible. "When you have an orgasm, you get a real flood of oxytocin and vasopressin. And these are the basic bodily and brain systems for attachment. Don't have sex with somebody you don't want to feel something for."[1] Fisher has never been a part of any form of organized religion, so these statements are based on her scientific research. She's not assigning a moral value to her conclusions, and we're not going to either.

Fisher's research (alongside that of many other scientists) shows that there's no such thing as casual sex. To understand this, we have to examine the biological processes that take place within our bodies when we have sex. First, please note that the processes happen in roughly the same way, regardless of your gender or orientation. Some hormonal and chemical reactions are determined by our biological sex, but those chemicals are not inherently gendered, at least when it comes to what happens during sexual activity. I'll be sure to tell you when biological sex differences are worth noting, but otherwise, don't worry about it.

Let me introduce to you two of my friends, Alex and Frankie, who conveniently have gender-neutral names and who also don't actually exist. Alex could be you. Or Frankie. Take your pick.

Alex and Frankie are both single but don't want to stay that way. One day, Alex is flipping through a dating app and runs across Frankie's photo. Alex feels that little rush of desire, a slight flutter, and exclaims, "Cuuuuute!" Alex quickly flips through all of Frankie's photos. That little flutter of attraction is testosterone—yes, the same hormone that we usually associate with masculinity. Turns out, testosterone is what Fisher calls "the hormone of sexual desire,"[2] and it's at the core of our feelings of sexual attraction and sexual desire, regardless of our biological sex. The more testosterone we have, the more strongly and more often we experience desire. The less we have, the fewer sexual feelings we experience. And in case you're wondering—no, low testosterone doesn't correlate with asexuality; that's a whole different thing.

Alex swipes right. It's a match! The excitement Alex feels is dopamine, the chemical of pleasure, and its primary purpose is to activate the reward system in our brain. Nearly everything that feels good activates dopamine—not just sexual pleasure, but any pleasure. Eating cake, seeing that we've gotten a text message, hugging our dogs—that warm, fuzzy, feel-good feeling is dopamine, and it's great. Whenever we feel dopamine, our brains immediately want more. Dopamine signals goodness to our brains, and we will do whatever we can to feel it over and over and over again.

As Alex and Frankie start chatting and get to know each other, they're each experiencing the complex interplay between dopamine and testosterone, which function as a feedback loop: dopamine produces more testosterone, and vice versa. As both increase, so does sexual desire.

Eventually, Alex and Frankie meet up for a date. Their attraction holds up in real life, and they move closer to each other as the evening goes on, with Frankie brushing Alex's arm every once in a while, and Alex moving close enough so their knees touch.

These touches produce oxytocin, the chemical responsible for providing calming feelings. Oxytocin suppresses our stress hormones, which are called cortisol and adrenaline. When oxytocin is flowing, we feel less stressed and more at ease. It's the chemical that makes us feel close to someone, producing feelings of trust and calm. Alex and Frankie's little touches begin to build higher levels of oxytocin in both of their brains, helping them relax and also producing more dopamine. They're both starting to feel really good.

Their first date ends with a good, long kiss—dopamine, testosterone, and oxytocin are pumping through their brains. As they say goodnight, they're both feeling a little bit light-headed, because all three of these chemicals can plummet almost as quickly as they rise, leaving our brains wanting a bit more and producing mild withdrawal effects. They both decide that they can't wait long to see each other again.

Soon, Alex and Frankie decide to jump into bed together and have sex. Their foreplay slowly begins to build dopamine and oxytocin, and another chemical is introduced: vasopressin, which is similar to oxytocin. As intercourse begins, these chemicals flood their brains, building pleasure upon pleasure upon pleasure. And as they climax, every one of these chemicals spikes. Dopamine increases 400 percent during an orgasm with another person. Oxytocin and vasopressin, the hormones of connection and calm, are also the hormones of attachment, and they peak to extreme levels during orgasm as well.

When these chemicals mix in Alex's and Frankie's brains and course through their bodies, they produce feelings of intense pleasure. These chemicals spike during *every* orgasm, but only half as high during masturbation as when we're with another person. Likely, Alex and Frankie don't orgasm together (it's very rare for people to orgasm together), but as soon as their respective orgasms are over, the chemical levels plummet, leaving Alex and Frankie breathless.

As soon as these chemicals disappear from their brains, a new chemical, called prolactin, rushes in to replace them. Prolactin is the hormone that makes us feel satisfied. Prolactin also is a dopamine inhibitor, meaning that when prolactin is around, dopamine is not. Higher levels of prolactin equal lower levels of dopamine. Prolactin makes us feel satisfied and satiated. For biologically male people, prolactin is the chemical that makes us feel sleepy after sex.

Whew. Got it?

Of course, we're only scratching the surface here, but this is enough of a basic overview for us to use our knowledge about these chemicals as we try to define our sexual ethics. Flip back to the resource section to find a list of some incredible books I recommend highly that describe these processes in more detail.

ALL IN THE CHEMICALS

The chemicals released during sexual activity are chemicals of pleasure. Testosterone sparks attraction and desire, working alongside dopamine as we interact with the person we're attracted to. Oxytocin and vasopressin jump into the action next, helping us feel calm and connected by suppressing our stress hormones, cortisol and adrenaline. If cortisol and adrenaline stick around because they're preventing dopamine and oxytocin from suppressing them, we don't enjoy sex as much, or we may be unable to have sex. These are the chemicals of our flight/fight/freeze response—an alarm system that might be triggered when we've experienced trauma.

If we've had sexual experiences with people who have made us feel unsafe or who have perpetrated violence against us, it's harder for our bodies to dial down our stress hormones; instead, they can be heightened. While this response is potentially scary and frustrating, our bodies are working precisely the way they're supposed to, telling us, "Be careful here. This might cause us harm." Cortisol and adrenaline can also be present as a result of the messages that we've been told about sex, such as that sex outside of a certain context is dangerous. They prevent us from feeling arousal. These chemicals explain why people who have grown up with a sexual ethic that says, "Don't have sex outside of marriage, or else," might have trouble having sex, even once they're married.

These stress hormones, unfortunately, don't just magically disappear on command, even if we've worked through our shame. We have to manage them with new experiences, practice, time, and often the help of a good therapist.[3]

When we jump in bed with someone (and our stress hormones don't put the brakes on), dopamine, oxytocin, and vasopressin all surge. They build and build and build until there's sudden release. In the moment of orgasm, extreme amounts of oxytocin, vasopressin, and dopamine flood the brain, and then, in the absence of more stimulation, they stay around for about five minutes. In biological men, even with more stimulus, these hormones almost immediately begin to plummet as prolactin rises. Sometimes biological men can have multiple orgasms, but this usually requires significant effort. For biological women, the hormones stay heightened, affording women a better chance of having multiple orgasms. The more orgasms a woman has, the more prolactin is eventually produced. The key word here is *eventually*. Men experience a prolactin spike almost immediately; women do not.

At some point, all the fun stops, and dopamine goes away. Prolactin replaces it, and eventually that fades, too, and we're back to where we started. Yet, the chemicals oxytocin and vasopressin stay in the mix in some additional ways.

Oxytocin and vasopressin are hormones that build over time with repeated interaction and release suddenly during intercourse. They are our hormones of attachment, and attachment as a whole also builds over time. As we have experiences with our romantic partners, including brief touches, hugs, and sex, our baseline levels of oxytocin and vasopressin increase. The more oxytocin and vasopressin in our systems, the more we feel secure, calm, trusting, and connected to our partners. As these feelings increase, cortisol decreases. But that build doesn't happen suddenly; it's a slow process occurring over months and years. During an orgasm, hormones spike suddenly, as we saw earlier, by roughly 400 percent. This spike can contribute to building our baseline of connection with a person, or it can be a one-time event. Regardless, the spike of these incredibly powerful hormones affects us, no matter what our baseline is.

Remember, prolactin is a dopamine inhibitor, meaning that once our prolactin levels go up after sex, we will feel satisfied and satiated, but we may no longer feel as good. Prolactin functions to shut off our sexual desire. Think of it as the body's brakes to all the testosterone and dopamine flooding our brains. As our dopamine levels decrease, the high feeling that dopamine gives us goes away.

Just like Alex and Frankie after their kiss, we can then experience slight withdrawal symptoms, which lead some of us to feel depressed, argumentative, or just kind of yucky. These feelings can be counteracted by having a higher baseline level of oxytocin and vasopressin, but if that baseline isn't there and if we're paying attention, we're probably going to feel a little bit off after having sex.

This feeling of withdrawal can begin a cycle in which we find ourselves needing another hit of dopamine to feel good again. We might then start using sex to soothe ourselves with dopamine as a way to fill an ever-growing gap caused by the sudden spikes and decreases in oxytocin and vasopressin in our brains. Instead of sex being fulfilling and satisfying, we get caught up in a cycle of constant hookups to avoid the deeper feelings lying underneath. We're going to talk more about this cycle in the next chapter.

THE POTENTIAL OF CONNECTION

All of the chemicals we've been describing work together toward one thing: connection. Even dopamine plays a part in this, keeping us returning for more (until it doesn't anymore, but that's also for the next chapter). When we have sex with someone, we can't stop these processes from happening in our brain and in our bodies; they're unavoidable, and they affect us no matter what. Yes, even you. Because any time we come into contact with another human being, any time we come into the *presence* of another human being, we are affected. That's simply the way we're wired; like the earth creature in the garden of Eden, we cannot exist alone.

So if the chemicals that are released during sex all work toward the same goal of connection, then it's starting to become clear why there's no such thing as casual sex. The idea of no-strings-attached sex is untenable because these chemicals *are* strings; they're strings that connect us to the people who are helping to produce these chemicals in our bodies. If connection is an inevitable by-product of sex, then the risk that sex carries can be summed up in two words: broken connection.

Now, this is the point where the youth pastor voice in our heads (let's name him Tim) concludes, "So, therefore, you should only ever have sex with one person, after you're married." Period. End of story. Right?

Wrong. Tim the Youth Pastor assumes two things: (1) a broken connection is inevitable; and (2) we don't have any kind of control over the ways sex connects us. Neither one of these assumptions is true.

Broken connection can be incredibly painful. Many of us know what it's like to share a sexual connection with someone and never hear from them again. We know the pain of a broken heart after a breakup. Researchers have demonstrated that pain from a broken heart has the same physiological effects as a bodily injury. It affects us deeply. And if sex creates connection, then it also increases the possibility of broken connection.

But broken connection is different from disconnection. And I'm proposing that by understanding the biological realities of sex, we will be able to mitigate the risk of broken connection and instead have a choice in the ways we disconnect.

THE TRUST FLOOR

The first strategy for mitigating the risk of broken connection hinges on our hormonal wiring: building our oxytocin and vasopressin floor. I'll call this a "trust floor." Because these are the chemicals of attachment, the chemicals that make us feel calm and connected, building this floor in a relationship allows us to get over the prolactin slump more effectively. It's pretty easy to do, because our trust floor is formed by spending time with our partner. Those little touches, kissing, sharing the details of our day, cuddling on the couch—all of these things build our trust floor, and it happens over time. Research shows that the less of a trust floor we have established in our relationships, the more likely sex will lead to broken connection instead of furthered connection.

New sexual relationships are built primarily on testosterone and dopamine, which contribute to the warm, fuzzy feelings we get when we are with a person we really like. They kick off the euphoric honeymoon phase. When we jump into bed with someone and have sex, our bodies naturally dampen the very chemicals that our relationship is initially built on. We may wake up the next morning trying to feel that euphoric high, the good feelings that come when we're around that person, only to find that they are gone. Prolactin inhibits dopamine. And if we don't have that trust floor built up, there's not much left, chemically speaking anyway, for our relationship to stand on.

Waiting to have sex until a relationship is solid outside the bedroom gives our trust floor the chance to develop. It allows us to work *with* our biological wiring instead of against it. Now, there are plenty of people who have sex early on in a relationship and go on to have fulfilling, long-term relationships. Tim the Youth Pastor wants to take this information and put a value statement on it, warning us, "If you have sex with someone early in a relationship, you will break up."

As we've learned, though, there are no easy if-then correlations in sexual matters. Because of the amounts of oxytocin and vasopressin released during sex, sex is a very effective way of building that trust floor, too. But if we're not starting with some trust, we're going to have to deal with the prolactin slump. The answers aren't simple.

Some of us may decide to wait to have sex with someone we really like until there's a bit more of that trust floor established. For others, this information helps us know what to expect if we choose to jump in bed early on in a relationship. We're able to anticipate our reactions and respond appropriately. The post-sex prolactin spike doesn't have to mean the end of a relationship, but it does mean that after having sex, we might suddenly start realizing that we don't like our partner as much as we thought we did.

Remember my client Hannah from chapter 2? I told her it might be time to make a few mistakes. Two weeks into the relationship she had started after I said this, she wasn't feeling the way she wanted to about the girl. All the red flags were still there, and they didn't seem to be going away, but she had already introduced her partner to her friends, and she really wanted things to work out. She was so excited to be in a relationship, with her first girlfriend, the end of being single. But something didn't feel right. She decided that if this relationship was going to happen, she needed to figure out how to feel close and connected to this girl. Maybe sex was the solution.

So at the two-week mark of this relationship, Hannah had sex for the first time, and it didn't make her feel the way she hoped it would. She broke up with her the next day.

The dopamine Hannah's sexual partner had produced

in her was already starting to wear off before they had sex, and she had found herself being less and less attracted to her as time went on. Having sex, while spiking dopamine for a minute, effectively wiped out any residual feelings of excitement and novelty that having a girlfriend had been producing in her. What was left was the cold, hard truth: she didn't like this girl. They had no floor of trust, no floor of safety and comfort. She wasn't the kind of girl Hannah wanted to date, and her friends didn't like her—even though they had tried to pretend they did.

The morning after having sex, Hannah sat in her apartment, sipping coffee and staring out the window. Instead of feeling closer together as a result of their physical intimacy, she felt even farther apart. Hannah felt a lot of shame about this in our next session. Instead of connecting them, their sexual adventure was the last thread in an unraveling relationship. Yet this seems paradoxical: in some ways, they *were* closer together, thanks to the bonding effects of oxytocin and vasopressin. They were connected in a different way than they had been before they had sex, but not in the way they needed for a lasting relationship.

What happened to Hannah and her girlfriend speaks to the power of these chemicals and the complexity they introduce. These chemicals, which have the potential to bring connection and deeper relationship, can also push us further away from each other, depending on the context and combination. By being aware of the way the chemicals interact and our motivations behind having sex, we can make better-informed choices about jumping into bed. Knowing that there are incredibly complex chemical processes happening right underneath the surface gives us understanding about why we may feel what we do.

As I explained some of these processes to Hannah, it

helped her move from "I am a bad person for having sex," a position of shame, to understanding why she had made the decision to have sex and why she immediately broke off the relationship afterward. She was not bad for having sex. She wasn't bad for wanting connection. But the connection she was yearning for wasn't going to be met by having sex in this context. In fact, having sex worked against her goal; they would have needed to have built a trust floor first.

But what about sex that we don't *want* to lead to a deeper connection? What if we don't want to build a trust floor with someone and just want to hook up? Understanding the science of sex can be empowering in these situations as well. If we approach hookups with the understanding that they will connect us, we will be in a better place to work with ourselves and the relationship to avoid painful broken connections. Two things will help: boundaries and communication.

Boundaries and communication are the foundation of consent, which is an absolute nonnegotiable for healthy sex. It's vital for the flourishing of people we come into contact with, especially for our sexual partners. Clear mutual communication, clear agreement, and clear boundaries all support consent.

Boundaries are clarified simply, Brené Brown writes, as "our lists of what's okay and what's not okay."[4] This can range from talking about what kind of sex you're going to have, to deciding on that together, to talking about what is going to happen after the hookup. There are limitless possibilities here, but what's important is that everyone is clear on what's going to happen and what each person's expectations are. If you decide you don't want to put firm limits on how things will go, then be clear about that, and commit to keeping the lines of communication open throughout your encounter so that you can adapt and adjust as needed. If everyone is on the same page from the start, that will help mitigate misunderstandings and broken connection.

If the hookup is going to be a one-time thing, make that clear at the beginning. It's as easy as saying, "I really want to have sex with you, but I don't want to build a relationship. This is a one-time thing for me; is that okay with you?" If you change your mind and decide you would like to have sex again, then simply talk about that. Being clear prevents any surprises.

These conversations should be happening whether we're preparing for a hookup or we're in a relationship. Expectations change, likes and dislikes change, moods change. Even if you've had sex with the same person hundreds of times, you don't truly know where your partner is at any given moment. As these changes are discussed, as communication stays open and healthy, your sex life can get better and better.

Communication and boundaries create the context for flourishing. They make it possible for sex to reach its good and healthy potential. When I'm preparing to go hiking with my friends, understanding the risks allows us to make our experience so much better, so much more fun. It doesn't guarantee that things won't go wrong, but it does allow us to navigate and be prepared. In the same way, by understanding the complexities of sex and by communicating with our partners what those complexities mean for us, we enable ourselves to mitigate risk and have truly good sex.

But the conversations this preparation requires us to have, like sex in general, can be difficult, because they make us vulnerable. It can be hard to admit to someone that we only want to have sex with them once. It can be hard to communicate clearly our expectations and our desires, even if we have built a strong trust floor. Sex is an inherently vulnerable act, and that's what we'll explore next.

Notes

1. Helen Fisher, "This Is Your Brain on Sex," interview by Krista Tippett, *On Being*, February 12, 2015, updated April 5, 2018, https://tinyurl.com /y4vex5cn.
2. Helen Fisher, *Why We Love: The Nature and Chemistry of Romantic Love* (New York: Henry Holt, 2004), 53.
3. When it comes to sexual harm and sexual trauma, there is a great deal of complexity that is beyond the scope of this book. Two other books may be helpful here: Emily Nagoski, *Come as You Are: The Surprising New Science That Will Transform Your Sex Life* (New York: Simon & Schuster, 2015); and, from a more traditionally Christian perspective, Dan B. Allender, *Healing the Wounded Heart: The Heartache of Sexual Abuse and the Hope of Transformation* (Grand Rapids: Baker, 2016). If at some point you want to seek the help of a therapist who has experience working with sexual abuse and trauma, I highly recommend the Allender Center's online directory.
4. Brené Brown, *Rising Strong: How the Ability to Reset Transforms the Way We Live, Love, Parent, and Lead* (New York: Random House, 2017), 126.

CHAPTER 8.

PARADOX 2: SEX MAKES US VULNERABLE AND HELPS US AVOID VULNERABILITY

A few weeks after my friend Bobby's first real heartbreak, he pulled himself out of bed long enough to make the trek up Capitol Hill to our friend Abbye's apartment. She had rightly intuited that he needed a break from the endless journaling and crying he had been filling his days with and coaxed him out of his blanket nest with the promise of a good bottle of wine and a homemade dinner.

As they sat in her apartment with its vast windows overlooking the night lights of the Seattle skyline, Bobby poured out his heart to her. He sat wrapped up in another blanket, alternating between the frozen pizza she had put in the oven, his wine, and the salad she was forcing him to eat. Everything flowed out: all his big feelings, how stupid it was that he got his heart into this mess, and how much he missed his ex.

After listening for a while, Abbye shifted the conversation: "We need to go dancing, and you need to wear something that you feel good in."

"I didn't bring any clothes." Bobby wasn't about to be coaxed out of yet another blanket nest.

"How about these?" Abbye held up a pair of heels, "I'm pretty sure we have the same foot size."

Bobby looked at her in shock. This wasn't exactly the way he had expected the night to go, but now that she mentioned it, a night in a dark club did sound like it might do wonders. Bobby tried on the heels and took his first shaky steps with a view five inches higher than he was used to. Bobby looked hot. Abbye threw on some Beyoncé. "This isn't going to fix things," she acknowledged, "but it is going to distract you."

They took a few selfies, posted them on Instagram because Bobby *knew* his ex was still watching, and walked out into the rainy Seattle night. As he clomped up the hill, getting used to all the new muscles that were required to walk in heels, stumbling and slipping, he began to laugh. Abbye was right. This was working.

"What would be the best thing that could happen for you tonight?" Abbye asked. "If you could do anything, what would you do?"

Bobby paused to take a breath, "I want to have fun."

Abbye shot him a look to make it clear that wasn't nearly enough.

"OK, fine. I want to make out with someone."

"Louder."

"I want to make out with a random man at the club!" Bobby yelled into the rain.

She laughed. "Yes, there it is. Let's go make that happen."

BEING WOUNDED

"Vulnerability" is a buzzword, a word that almost seems to have lost its meaning because of how often it comes up in casual conversation. Ever since Brené Brown's 2010 TEDx Talk on "The Power of Vulnerability" introduced mainstream culture to the concept of vulnerability as the antidote to shame, it seems we can't go a day without someone writing something "really vulnerable" on

Facebook with the expectation of becoming a viral sensation because of their "brave authenticity."

So, let's get on the same page. What do we really mean when we talk about vulnerability? My favorite definition, because of its simplicity, comes from a Canadian doctor and trauma expert named Gabor Maté, who defines vulnerability as "our susceptibility to be wounded."[1]

The first time I read that definition, I felt as if Maté had punched me in the gut. The definition seemed so obvious, but I had never seen vulnerability defined in such stark terms before. It's not just an uncomfortable feeling or a feeling of being uncertain about how people might respond to us, and it's not just feeling exposed, although these are all definitely part of being vulnerable. Vulnerability is opening ourselves up to being *wounded*. Vulnerability means knowing we might not get out of a situation without being hurt but choosing to go there anyway.

As my working definition in this chapter, I'll use this: vulnerability is our capacity to be wounded, our willingness to be influenced, and our choices that lead to the potential of being hurt. I would imagine you're already drawing connections between vulnerability and our sex lives, because there are very few more vulnerable things we can do with another person than get undressed and share physical and emotional intimacy. There's so much potential for being wounded, in so many different ways, and many of us have experienced that wounding firsthand. We know what it's like to be hurt, and in turn, we know what it's like to respond to that pain by putting up barriers of protection.

That's the paradox here—our second paradox about sex. Sex is at the same time one of the most vulnerable experiences we can have and one of our most commonly used tools for avoiding vulnerability. From our masturbation and fantasy lives to our hookups to our committed relationships and marriages, we can use sex as a means to further connection, or we can use it to avoid connection altogether. Understanding how this paradox works in our lives is another step toward overcoming our sexual shame, because when we know what we're doing and why we're doing it, we're less likely to be attacked by our shame voices.

That night with Abbye, Bobby did end up finding a random guy to make out with. Later, as he walked home with Abbye—leaning on her because the heels were making it impossible to walk—Bobby felt he was back in the game. While he still had months of healing from his heartbreak ahead of him, that little spike of dopamine was what he needed. Abbye had succeeded in distracting him from his heartbreak, and he felt great.

Using the dopamine spike from making out with someone to avoid or heal some vulnerability is not a bad thing. I don't want us to put value judgments on avoiding vulnerability, as if somehow being constantly vulnerable makes us "good" and avoiding it makes us "bad." Sometimes we use the concept of vulnerability like a weapon, which only perpetuates our shame. If we're thinking back to all the times we've used sex or alcohol or food to avoid feeling our pain, placing a moral judgment on those experiences does nothing but intensify our shame. As we talk about vulnerability, be aware of how sneakily those shame voices can jump in.

WIRED FOR NOVELTY

You'll remember from the previous chapter that when we have sex, dopamine spikes, which makes us feel good—like, *really* good. Those few sweet minutes of a dopamine rush are like nothing else; they're an escape from all the hard and complicated feelings of the world.

Here's the thing about dopamine, though: one of its primary functions is to make us want more. Usually, our first spike of dopamine is the best. For example, when we go to a restaurant and try a new dessert for the first time, that first bite is simply magical. So we go on for the second bite, and the third, and about the time we hit the fourth or fifth bite, the magic has worn off. By the time we are finished with the dessert, that moment of bliss from the first bite is only a vague memory.

This happens with sex, too. We are wired for novelty, for new situations, new circumstances. Novelty combined with dopamine equals something delicious in our brains, and it's what makes the fireworks pop. It also means that in the absence of novelty, once we get used to something or someone, our dopamine levels don't spike as much. It's why the excitement of sex fades in a long-term relationship or marriage. The novelty, or what some people call the honeymoon phase, wears off. In our sexual relationships, this is called the Coolidge effect. It's an effect that most of us have experienced in our lives, even if we're not sexually active. It's similar to what happens when we return to a place where we once had an incredible experience, only to find that it doesn't live up to our expectations a second time. We get a little bit disappointed, and we apologize to our friends for talking it up so much.

The Coolidge effect is observed in the animal kingdom, including in humans. Its basic principle is that we get much more sexual excitement from someone new than from someone we've been with before. Here's an easy way to remember the Coolidge effect: it sounds like "cool age," which is an apt description of what happens. Sexual excitement cools proportionately with the age of the relationship.

I assumed that the effect was discovered by some scientist named Coolidge and thought, "How convenient is that?" Yet when I looked into it, I found my assumption was wrong. It was named not after a scientist, but after a US presidential couple, Calvin and Grace Coolidge, who were in the White House from 1923 to 1929. The story goes that during Calvin Coolidge's presidency, Calvin and Grace were invited to tour a new experimental government farm. They split up for the tour, and as Grace entered the chicken yard, she noticed a particularly horny rooster, who was getting it on with hen after hen. Grace, who I imagine being quite charming, pointed out the rooster and asked her tour guide how often he mated with the hens.

"Dozens of times each day."

Grace nodded her head and smiled, "Please tell that to the president when he comes by."

The tour guide did indeed tell Calvin, who asked, "Same hen every time?"

"Oh, no, a different one every time."

"Tell that to Grace, please."

In 1958, behavioral endocrinologist Frank Beach first wrote about the fact that among some animals, males are sexually attracted to many *new* partners, even though their attraction to a previous partner has disappeared. He called it the Coolidge effect.

In humans, when sex becomes less exciting as time goes on, people strive to "spice things up a little bit" in marriages and long-term relationships. I see this in my clients all the time. My client Emma, for example, often complained about her lack of a sex life with her wife. Once she understood the Coolidge effect, she and her wife got a little bit more adventurous in bed and even started experimenting with bringing someone else into the mix on occasion.

Dopamine lessens over time unless faced with novelty; this is known as tolerance. This pattern is often recognized as a particularly male characteristic. Think of the cliché image of a man whose midlife crisis manifests in an affair with his secretary. But there's research emerging that the Coolidge effect is just as common among women.

I think of the Coolidge effect as being similar to our prolactin response after sex, but on a more long-term basis. Both of these phenomena reduce the levels of dopamine we produce. Both dampen the soothing, pleasurable effects of dopamine and, indirectly, open us up to all the other feelings that might come flooding in: discomfort, anxiety, dread, grief—everything we often try to avoid. Dopamine helps mitigate the effects of those feelings, often allowing us to eliminate them for some time. But when the dopamine fades, we're back to sitting with those feelings again. And what's the easiest way to get rid of those feelings?

Another dopamine hit.

And another.

And another.

We see this happening in the coping mechanisms of shamefulness and shamelessness, as we talked about in the first few chapters of this book. When we cope through shamefulness, we're sexually active within secrecy, and there's a good chance we're using the dopamine rush to help us manage our shame. When we cope through shamelessness, there's no doubt we're using dopamine as a way to mitigate the fact that we haven't actually dealt with the shame hiding underneath. These mechanisms are at the heart of how we use sex to avoid vulnerability.

AVOIDING VULNERABILITY

Anytime we jump into bed with someone as a way to help ourselves feel better, or after a fight with our partner, or to avoid conflict, or without working through what actually happened to trigger this response, we're using sex to avoid vulnerability. In other words, when our quest for a dopamine hit serves the function of avoiding connection or as a *shortcut* to connection—either connection with ourselves and our own feelings, or connection with another person—again, we're using sex to avoid vulnerability.

While the chemicals that are released during sex—primarily the oxytocin and vasopressin—are the chemicals of attachment, we can consciously cut off or avoid the parts of ourselves that feel that connection. But when we cut off one part of ourselves, we cut off many others as well. We cannot choose to be unaffected by our sexual encounters without putting up walls in other parts of our lives too.

In the hit TV series *How I Met Your Mother*, the story arc of the character Barney Stinson illustrates this principle well. For the first few seasons of the show, we learn that Barney loves having sex—a lot of sex, with as many different women as possible. Through the course of the show, Barney has sex with hundreds of women.

Barney always laughs off his encounters, hatching elaborate plans in order to hook up with girls and then just as elaborate plans to leave them hanging the next morning. It's sex with no strings attached, or so it seems. His friends at times seem baffled by his ability to remain unaffected. But throughout the seasons, we notice Barney getting more and more desperate, eventually looking for a long-term relationship but not being able to find one. His girlfriends always eventually leave him.

Finally, in one of the later seasons of the show, Barney finds a girl he falls in love with, and he risks opening up to her. In a memorable moment, Barney shares with his best friend, Ted, that all the sex he has had over the last years "left me feeling nothing but—but broken. But now, for the first time in my life, I feel settled, and happy. I wanna feel this way forever."[2] By opening himself to the vulnerability of connection, Barney was able to break down some of his walls and experience actual intimacy, actual connection. As he did that, his relationship thrived.

We are wired for connection. Sex is primarily about connection. When we actively keep ourselves from experiencing the connection that inevitably happens during a sexual encounter, we are numbing every other part of ourselves. We are reducing our capacity for connection as a whole.

Simply stated, sex without vulnerability is self-serving. We do it because we want to feel better, because we really need to get off, or because we're lonely. We use it to avoid tough conversations and to make up after arguments. We use it early on in relationships because it's easier than wading into vulnerability by opening up to another person. Having sex early in a relationship is not a bad thing if we're aware of what we're doing, but it becomes damaging when we have sex instead of facing the reality of our pain, our shame, and the things we're trying to avoid.

In today's world, it's easy to avoid facing our own selves by turning instead to sex on demand through our phones. And again, to belabor the point, hooking up via an app is *not a bad thing*, but we need to be aware of why we are doing it and the emotional risks.

Sex can be just as much about avoiding connection as it can be about connection. Yet when we use it to avoid connection, it throws our brains and bodies for a loop, and we often end up feeling even worse than before we had sex. Thus, we are faced with a choice: either actually deal with what we're running away from or look for another dopamine spike. This happens in committed relationships just as often as it happens for single people.

It happens in our masturbation lives just as often as it happens when we hook up.

THE SECRET WEAPON

In a relationship built on a trust floor of oxytocin and vasopressin, the Coolidge effect still applies. Over time, sex may not feel as exciting, but thanks to the trust floor, it has a different quality—one that still produces a dopamine rush (just not as extreme) and also provides a much more fulfilling experience. This is the secret weapon of long-term relationships: even if we jump to sex to avoid uncomfortable feelings, eventually we have to come face-to-face with our feelings and our partner. That encounter then produces even more oxytocin and vasopressin. Attachment bonds are strengthened.

When we hook up, that's not the case—making it all the more essential for us to be aware of our internal motivations. This way, we aren't under any delusions about sex making things better, and instead we can enjoy it for what it is: a dopamine rush that will soon be followed by having to face ourselves again. Along with that, we potentially get a complicated situation with another person if we didn't set good boundaries.

Embracing vulnerability is possible in every sexual encounter we have, and it's as simple as letting ourselves be affected by the person we are with. Sex allows us to connect in powerful ways, and we literally sync up with another person, gaining a level of intimacy that not only tells us a lot about the person we are with, but also tells us a lot about ourselves. Paying attention to these experiences instead of avoiding them is the key to not cutting off our capacity for connection. This means that when we hook up, we must let ourselves feel connected to the person we're hooking up with and then work with the emotions that emerge as a result.

Based on our relationship patterns, some of us will have a harder time with the idea of a casual hookup. Others of us have the ability to connect with another person momentarily, feel that connection, and then move on. It is crucial that if hookups are going to be a part of our sexual ethics, we get to know exactly how we respond to these momentary connections. What feelings do they bring up in us when we're with each new person? What happens to us after we say good-bye? What are all the feelings that come flooding in once prolactin spikes and we're no longer feeling the effect of dopamine? For some of us, hookups are going to affect us too profoundly to be able to engage in them in a healthy way; they bring up too many emotions. For others, there will be few or no problems.

Each of us is different. If we're reaching for sexual health and freedom from sexual shame, it's essential to be aware of how we're feeling. If it doesn't feel healthy, if it doesn't produce positive, enjoyable, pleasurable results, then it's *not sexual health*. In that case, we would do much better to express our sexuality within the safety of a long-term relationship—having established a solid trust floor. That's where we're going next.

Notes

1. Gabor Maté, *In the Realm of Hungry Ghosts: Close Encounters with Addiction* (Berkeley, CA: North Atlantic, 2010), 40.

2. *How I Met Your Mother*, season 8, episode 11, "The Final Page: Part One," directed by Pamela Fryman, written by Dan Gregor and Doug Mand, aired December 17, 2012, on CBS.

CHAPTER 9.

PARADOX 3: SEX REQUIRES SAFETY AND SAFETY IS NOT GUARANTEED

"Oh, my god, I forgot to re-park the car." Alvin's whisper broke through the darkness, and Jack rolled over to look at the man in his bed, who he was just beginning to get used to calling his boyfriend. It was one in the morning. They were trying the long-distance thing. Alvin had arrived earlier that night, and they spent the evening with Jack's sister, who also was visiting. Everyone was packed into Jack's tiny studio apartment, his sister soundly sleeping on the couch a few feet from his bed; their whispers were barely audible.

Jack told me this story a few years later. He explained that Denver has weird street-parking rules, probably no different from any other city, and the two men didn't want to spend upwards of $25 a day to park Alvin's car near his apartment. He had suggested to Alvin that they move it to a neighborhood north of his where street parking was free.

"I'll come with you." Jack whispered to Alvin. They hadn't had any alone time yet, and this seemed like a perfect opportunity to make up for a couple of weeks of not seeing each other.

"It's so late," Alvin whispered back. "Just tell me where I need to go, and I'll be back soon."

Jack tried to make eye contact. "No, I'll come with you. So we can, you know . . . away from her."

Alvin got it.

Warm yellow light from the downtown buildings lit their faces as they moved through the darkness to his car. They drove up a hill to find a parking space and began to make out. A few weeks before, Jack and Alvin had decided they didn't want to have sex for a long time, but frequent make-out sessions had become the way they spent the majority of their time together.

Jack caught Alvin's gaze as they came up for air, his brown eyes illuminated by the warmth of the streetlights. "I feel so safe with you," Alvin whispered to Jack, laying his head on his chest. Jack ran his fingers through Alvin's hair and thought, "This is it. This is what I've been waiting years for. Safety. Yes."

Safety wasn't a word Jack would have chosen to describe the feeling, but the moment Alvin said it, Jack knew he felt it, too. There was something about the two of them together that eased his fears. Describing it to me, Jack recalled, "The insecurities that usually popped up in between conversations, the ways my mind played tricks on me would somehow disappear when he was close." During that time in the car, Jack felt his body settle and the warmth of ease wash over him. They had just made their relationship official a couple of weeks earlier—a first relationship for both of them—and at that moment, Jack knew it was going to be really good.

Except that it wasn't. Three days after their late-night rendezvous, they sat at a local pub, sharing a flight of beer. "I think we're in different places, and I don't know if I want to do this," Alvin said after taking a long sip of his stout.

Jack stared at him in shock, feeling the burger he had just eaten turn sour in his stomach. "What do you mean?"

Alvin and Jack talked for the rest of the evening, discussing what had been happening between them over the previous few weeks. Alvin said he wasn't actually sure he was ready to be in a relationship. As Jack later told me, he felt like he "was floating outside of myself." He couldn't believe what was happening.

Then, after a last kiss on the street corner, Alvin got in his car, and Jack knew he wasn't going to see Alvin again. The safety Jack had felt so recently before then was shattered.

Psychologists and psychotherapists have debated for years the idea of safety within relationships. Some say what we call "safety" is an illusion. Our brains trick us into feeling safe to cope with the immense amount of vulnerability that is inherent in every relationship. They say it doesn't exist, that we can't ever know ourselves or other people well enough to be genuinely safe. In other words, any sense of safety we think we feel with another person is nothing more than an alluring construct that can shatter in a moment's notice.

Others say that safety is vital and that relationships and sex are impossible without a sense of safety. They propose that while risk is inherently a part of all relationships (because vulnerability and risk go hand in hand), there are many forces that create safety and trust between people. This trust, while it can be broken, is something that we can lean into. It is real because we make it real *together*.

Perhaps both perspectives are right. As humans, we are innately wired to search for safety. We spend our lives looking for places of belonging. Many of us try to find that with another person, but talk to anyone who has experienced a divorce or a significant breakup, and you'll quickly realize how little we actually know about the most important people in our lives. We can feel safe, seen, and held by a person in one moment. We can love and feel loved back. We can commit to a lifetime with that person and one day wake up to the realization that we don't know that person at all. All of a sudden, they are foreign—we barely recognize them.

This is our third paradox. Safety—emotional, physical, and spiritual—is vital for our survival. But the safer we feel with a person or a group of people, the riskier those relationships are. No matter our relationship status—committed, single, or somewhere in between—we will at some point inevitably experience the shattering of safety. Part of stepping into a more healthy sexuality is learning how to recover and cope with the shame that comes next. As we work toward developing our own sexual ethic, we have to contend with the complexity of safety and risk and with the paradox of their cohabitation in our lives.

THE IMPORTANCE OF SAFETY

Safety for *each partner* must be a core value of our sexual ethic. We have to account for safety in our physical sexual practices, and we have to consider the emotional safety of our partner(s) and ourselves. Safety is a prerequisite for intimate relationships. Similarly, safety is vital for sex and sexual arousal. Sex devoid of safety isn't really sex at all; it is abuse or rape.

The paradox comes in because we must admit that safety is ultimately an illusion and that all sexual relationships involve risk—including those in which we feel most safe. In some ways, the longer we are in a relationship with someone, especially an intimate relationship, the riskier it gets. That's not a fun fact. Relationships inherently make us vulnerable, and no matter how hard we try, every time we enter into relationship with another person, we relinquish some control. We cannot guarantee our own safety or the safety of our partners, and much of what we call "safe" is nothing more than an elaborate mind game. The good news is that armed with this knowledge about the nature of safety, we can be better prepared for any difficulties that may arise. If we are in a long-term relationship or if we want to be in one, we must understand the way safety works (and doesn't work) between people.

SEX AND SAFETY

Three basic principles are at work within the safety paradox: First, for sex to be healthy, it *must* be safe. Second, we cannot guarantee safety, no matter how hard we try. And third, safety *will* be shattered, and our work is to learn how to recover.

Psychologist Michael Bader affirms that "sexual fantasy and arousal are chiefly grounded in safety."[1] In other words, it's tough to experience sexual arousal without first experiencing safety. Of course, every body is different, and each of us will respond to sexual stimulation in different ways. And our responses are further complicated when talking about sexual abuse, which is beyond the scope of this book. But as a general rule, arousal is predicated on safety. Bader and other psychologists believe that sexual fantasies—the things that turn us on, either in private or with other people—can be boiled down to our need for safety. Even our "dangerous" fantasies are unconsciously structured toward safety.

For example, in a sexual fantasy of being dominated by a partner, it would seem on the surface that this fantasy has little to do with safety; after all, much of the sexual allure of domination is wrapped up in the apparent *loss* of safety. Someone else takes control, having their way with us, sometimes in violent and risky ways. What's safe about that?

When we consider the *function* of the fantasy, however, we see what is being accomplished within the arousal and how safety comes into play. First, we must ask why this particular fantasy is needed to achieve sexual arousal. What might be behind this fantasy? Many of our most private sexual fantasies are tied directly to our shame stories. We can learn a lot about our shame by paying attention to our sexual fantasies. In the case of domination, we might be motivated by the belief that we are too much, too high maintenance, and have too many needs. Or the inverse, that we are worthless. Our shame story may be something like this: "I am too much/not enough. If I express my desire, if I am too sexual, I will be overwhelming, and my partner will leave." The function of this domination fantasy is to make sexuality feel safe, as it removes all potential of being too much/not enough, because we are no longer in control. All desire and responsibility are placed upon our partner, who wants us so intensely that all we have to do is let it happen. Suddenly, we are free to feel arousal. We are safe because our shame story has been bypassed.

Obviously, this is not the only explanation for domination fantasies, and it bears repeating that sexual fantasies are not bad, even as they reveal a lot about our feelings of shame. For our purposes, the takeaway is that sexual arousal often depends on feeling safe and free enough from our internal messages of shame. This is because shame hijacks our sense of safety. Nothing turns off sexual arousal faster than feelings of shame that interrupt us while we are getting it on. If you're making out with someone and your shame voice suddenly butts in and says, "I'm not good enough for them," you're going to have a tough time staying aroused.

The world of fantasy is a psychological safety net built to protect us from ourselves. When we don't feel safe with ourselves first, it's hard for us to feel safe with others. It's not impossible, but it's much more challenging to trust others when we cannot trust ourselves.

A former client of mine, Leah, came into my office because she felt like there was a wall between her and everyone else. "I don't have any friends, just the people I work with. And I don't know if those are really friendships."

Leah detailed her life for me. She mostly spent her time at home or at work. Occasionally, she would go out with her coworkers for happy hour, but she told me she never felt like she could actually connect with them.

We began to discover that this wall she was describing wasn't just keeping her from making friends; it was keeping her from accessing her emotions, too. One day, she came into my office visibly frustrated. She had gone out with her coworkers for a drink a couple days before, and the same thing had happened. "I felt like I just sat in the background, watching them all having fun but not having any fun myself."

On a whim, I decided to ask a question I had been wondering about for a while. "Leah, this may sound like an intrusive question, and if you're not comfortable sharing this information with me, I understand." I had her attention, "How often do you masturbate?"

Leah's eyes widened. "Uh," she stumbled, "I don't do that."

"Never?"

"Never."

Over the next few weeks, I began to encourage Leah to try exploring her body. She was hesitant but open to the idea. She even seemed a little bit excited to try. At first, she didn't experience much, but as time went on, she began to find some pleasure in it.

"It felt so good!" she told me one week, after spending an entire hour with herself one evening. As Leah began to explore her body, and as she began to trust herself and notice the feelings that came with that, she slowly began to open up to and acknowledge the breadth of emotions that existed right underneath the surface of the wall she had described to me.

Leah wasn't comfortable experiencing the array of emotions that come with living life. She didn't feel safe, so she had constructed a wall that kept both herself and others out. But by exploring her body, she started to learn that she could trust herself. And as she did this work internally, her relationships began to transform as well. She started making friends.

One of the first things we can do to explore the implications of the safety paradox is to take time to explore our bodies. What turns us on? Where do our minds go when we're masturbating? What kinds of touch do we like? Where do we like it? For those of us who were taught to fear our bodies, it can be difficult to touch ourselves and to let arousal happen. There is shame in the act of experiencing pleasure. We may feel dirty, as if we're doing something inappropriate. To break the hold of shame, we can start by touching ourselves and observing our thought patterns, including the judgment that comes along—without judging ourselves for judging!

We should ask ourselves some leading questions: What would it mean to experience pleasure solely for the sake of pleasure? Can we allow ourselves to get lost within our bodies and the vast world of sensation? Answering these questions can take a lot of thought and work, because the shame voices that come with self-pleasure can feel insurmountable. But addressing these voices is one positive step toward overcoming fears related to our own sexual expression. Some of the resources listed at the end of the book can help with this.

BRINGING IN ANOTHER PERSON

When we bring someone else into our lives, issues around safety, risk, and shame can get much more complicated very quickly. Part of being sex positive is making sure that our sexual experiences are positive for everyone involved, and that doesn't happen by accident. Unfortunately, there's nothing about sex that's guaranteed to be pleasurable or positive.

Many of us who were raised in purity culture assume that once we start having sex, it will always be good. What no one mentions—at least not until we join marital counseling or couples' groups—is that having good sex takes some work, a hard lesson to learn after committing to someone. In many church communities, members are explicitly *guaranteed* good, passionate, pleasurable, positive sex upon getting married. But those guarantees are impossible to honor.

Whether we're single or partnered, in a long-term relationship or meeting up with someone for one night, we have to try to understand and work with someone else's sense of safety, both emotional and physical.

Emotional safety can be hard to put our finger on and describe, in part because it has the potential of changing quickly. We can feel perfectly safe with someone, and then unexpectedly, they say or do something to cause that sense of safety to disappear. Our oxytocin stops pumping, and we may have second thoughts and a heightened sense of risk. Sometimes the spark that diminishes our feelings of safety and connection—at times right in the middle of things—has nothing to do with our partner's words or actions. No matter what initiates the feelings, we often allow our fear or our shame voices to prevent us from interrupting or stopping the sexual experience. But if we brush our feelings aside and continue, the sexual experience can quickly go from positive to leaving us feeling violated. This can happen in marriages just as easily as it can happen when we're single.

It's important to recognize that a sudden change from feeling safe to feeling at risk can happen for our partners as well. We can be moving forward and say or do something that takes them to an entirely different place, but here's the thing: we may not be able to tell how they're feeling in the moment. Changes within us and within the people we are with happen quickly and often internally, so they're easy to hide. The result may be hidden, too, or out in the open: the sex is no longer positive, even if it remains physically pleasurable.

One Wednesday a few months ago, my client Christie sat down on the couch in my office with a big sigh. She and her wife, Jane, had been working on establishing more intimacy. She told me, "I initiated sex with Jane last night, and it went terribly."

A part of me was proud, because this was something we had been working on. Christie wasn't the best at asking for what she wanted. I sat and waited for Christie to continue. She said, "Things started out great. We were kissing on the couch after dinner. Then, all of a sudden, I said something, and everything changed. I don't even know what it was, but just like that, it was over."

What Christie had said innocently triggered a negative memory for Jane, and that immediately changed the entire moment. Jane wasn't able to talk about what had happened for her until later, but Christie felt guilty, even though she had no way of knowing.

Jane was able to speak up and stop things with Christie, but when these shifts in feelings of safety happen, many of us simply endure. Shame can stop us in our tracks, but we might decide it's worth bearing what's happening inside instead of stopping, because we are afraid of what it might mean about us if we ask our partner to stop. Of course, sex should not be something we have to endure or get through. It shouldn't be that way for our partners either, and Christie was wise in not pressuring Jane to continue.

Let's be very clear: when sex becomes anything less than consensual, it is a violation. It is no longer safe. This goes back to needing to have a sense of safety with ourselves first. If we can trust ourselves to say no when we need to say no, at the moment when we feel something shift within us, we are establishing a trust floor with ourselves. That floor allows us to experience our sex lives with more freedom and more enjoyment.

Knowing how difficult it is to speak up for ourselves, especially when we're in the middle of sexual activity we've already said yes to, also gives us awareness and responsibility for our partners. For sex to remain safe, we need to be checking in with our partner, keeping communication open. We should be in tune, aware of both our own and our partner's emotional and internal worlds. If we notice a shift in our partner, we should check in and craft a space where sharing about the experience *in the moment* feels natural and open.

Let me write you a permission slip to get through the difficult times. You have permission to speak. Say, "This is no longer working for me," or "I'd prefer if we were to stop."

Consent is an ongoing process, not a one-time event. Checking in at appropriate moments, with a few words —"Is this OK with you?" "Does this feel good?" "Are you comfortable with this?"—will enhance the experience, not take away from it, ensuring pleasure and positivity for everyone involved.

This is all easier said than done and hinges on our ability to recognize and speak to our own experience in the moment. We may not get this right every time. It will take practice. Jim, one of my clients, recognized this the hard way after going home with a guy he thought was cute but wasn't super excited about having sex with. After a couple of glasses of wine, Jim was much more willing to jump into bed, but the next morning, he called to schedule an emergency session because he couldn't quite figure out what had happened. It initially felt great, he said. He was into it, enjoying it, but then suddenly it didn't feel right anymore. There was a point in the evening when Jim said he knew he no longer wanted to be with this man, but they were already too far into the encounter for Jim to feel he could stop. As Jim described it, his partner seemed so into the moment that it felt mean and uncaring to stop at the height of arousal, so he didn't.

Jim told me he wasn't particularly shaken up about the situation, and it wasn't necessarily a big deal, but it also wasn't an experience he wanted to repeat. He said he was just talking to me to figure out what had really happened, but I stopped that train of thought: "It sounds like you stopped consenting, so no wonder you're trying to sort out your emotions."

Jim paused for a few seconds in the conversation and then told me he was shocked by how I'd described the situation. "But I did consent. I went home with him. I said yes; I continued saying yes. I told him things felt good."

"Did they?"

"No." Jim told me how it felt lying there, thinking about how he was ready for his partner to be done already, so Jim could go home. "You're right, it wasn't good. I was no longer consenting."

Jim felt he couldn't communicate that feeling in the moment. Instead of saying what was actually going on for him, he continued to pretend he was enjoying the sex, all the while thinking about what he needed to get done the next day, planning out the rest of his evening, and trying to will his partner to finish so he could just leave.

There's nothing unusual about Jim's experience. Most of us are naturally empathetic and caring people, and once we're in the middle of an experience, we often choose to push our own pleasure aside to ensure a positive experience for whomever we are with. But that's not healthy sex.

A corollary paradox to the safety and risk paradox is that sex requires us to be both selfless and selfish at the same time. If we're not being selfless, paying attention to all the cues our partner is giving us, having a deep concern for their pleasure and their experience, we risk doing harm. If we're not selfish, paying attention to our own bodies, our internal world, having a concern for our own pleasure and experience, we risk harm to ourselves. The interplay of selfishness and selflessness makes sex mutually good: your pleasure *and* my pleasure, my pleasure *and* your pleasure.

Jim's partner that night should have paid attention to the breadth of clues Jim was giving him that the sex wasn't good anymore. But many of those clues were nonverbal, and that makes things complicated. Jim felt guilty because even though he wasn't enjoying the sex, he kept saying it "felt great" because he didn't want his partner to feel bad. Yet if Jim's partner was truly attuned to him, he probably would have been able to notice that things weren't right.

When we're having sex, we have to be willing to truly attune ourselves to and truly pay attention to our partners, not only to what they're telling us verbally, but also to what they're telling us in other ways, too. If Jim's partner had attuned himself to Jim better, he might have been able to pause and say, "Hey, it seems like you might not be enjoying this anymore. What can I do to help?"

It's easy to get wrapped up in one side or the other, choosing your own pleasure at the expense of someone else, or making sure someone else has a good experience at the expense of your own. It's much harder to do both at once, yet this is a vital part of emotional safety. We need to know that the person we are with is just as concerned for us as we are for ourselves and for them. This is true no matter the context of our relationship.

PHYSICAL SAFETY

Up until this point, we've been talking about forms of safety that are difficult to see but are very real. The most obvious kind of safety, though, and the one that is often talked about—but still not talked about enough—is physical safety.

In the world I grew up in, the idea of "safe sex"—practices that significantly reduce the health risks involved in having sex—was shunned. I often heard things like "The only safe sex is no sex at all." As a result, I had absolutely no sex education growing up. I didn't even know what a condom looked like until I was twenty. Many of my friends and clients have similar stories, which means that when we decide we're ready to have sex with someone, we're more likely to engage in unsafe sexual practices.

It is vital that we all understand how sexually transmitted infections work and the steps we can take to protect ourselves. As I write this book, we are on the brink of another HIV/AIDS crisis in the United States simply because there's a lack of understanding around safer-sex practices. This is true regardless of sexual orientation and regardless of whom we're having sex with.

This book isn't a safer-sex manual, so I encourage you to seek out more information on that topic, including the resources listed at the end of this book. But I can share a few questions that can guide your thinking about safer sex:

- Are we using protection?

- Are we taking the right medications based on how sexually active we are and based on our sexual orientations?

- Are we open with our doctors about what kinds of sex we are having and when?

- Are we sharing with our therapists about our sex lives and the resulting emotions?

Remember that your questions and issues are nothing your doctor and therapist haven't heard before. Professionals are trained for these conversations, and having someone to talk to openly who is concerned for your well-being can be extremely liberating. Ask more questions. If you're confused about how something works, speak up. You are in control of your own sexual health, so be informed.

But here's the deal. No matter how hard we try to be safe, no matter how much we try to protect ourselves from the inherent risks that come with connecting with another person in *any* way (not just sexual), safety is not guaranteed. That's the paradox.

Our youth pastors might have awkwardly warned us about the risks and dangers of sex, right after talking about their "smoking-hot wives." Their warnings ranged from "Condoms break" to "STIs still get transmitted" to "Guard your heart." There's a certain level of truth to these warnings. Condoms do break, and you can develop deep feelings for someone you're sleeping with who isn't worth it. So this is a further call for us to approach our sex lives with a level of intentionality, not a one-size-fits-all prescription for sex within marriage. Healthy sexual activity is going to look different for each of us.

THE FRAGILITY OF SAFETY

What our youth pastors didn't tell us was that once we're in a marriage, safety doesn't magically just appear. This is a hard and liberating truth. There's no such thing as a "safe" relationship. In fact, in some ways, marriage and commitment make a relationship less "safe" as time goes on.

When we're single, many of us dream about finding the perfect someone, someone who will make us feel loved and secure and wanted—someone we can do the little mundane things with, someone who will help us feel less alone in this world. We have dreams about that future relationship and the warm, fuzzy feelings that will come with it. I'm not here to shatter those dreams, because all of those things can and do happen when we find someone we want to spend a significant part of our lives with. However, just because we say a few vows or wake up one morning and realize that we've been living together for ten years doesn't mean the relationship is safe.

How many times have we heard statements like "I thought I knew him" or "I thought I knew everything about her, but it turns out I didn't" from people who have been in ten-, twenty-, thirty-year relationships after discovering something new about a person? Sometimes a person says, "I thought I knew" with delight, with awe. How wonderful that even after thirty years, there are new things to discover about this person we thought we knew. Other times, these words are said with despair and heartbreak. And when we've been in a relationship for significant periods of time, the heartbreak becomes that much harder to bear.

Remember our discussion of the trust floor? As we build that trust floor over years and years, as those chemicals of attachment build up, two things happen. First, by the time we've been in a relationship for that period of time, most of the dopamine has worn off. It takes effort to keep the spark alive. We might have the illusion that we know everything about a person. But we can never truly *know* another person. And it takes massive amounts of work to keep that relationship going. Some people do it successfully and say it's worth it. For others, that's not the case.

My friends Ralph and Lucy are a prime example of a couple who have managed to keep the spark alive. They've been married for over thirty years, have watched all their kids grow up, and are now back to living by themselves. Every time I see them, at some point, their sex life comes up. Lucy loves to talk about how Ralph *still* rocks her world after all these years. Ralph always looks very pleased with himself.

One of those times, I asked them what they've done to keep the spark alive after all these years. Lucy laughed. "Ralph still knows how to surprise me! I'm still learning new things about him!"

Ralph and Lucy have never been lulled into the idea that they know everything about each other; they're quite aware that they don't. They're still learning new things about each other every day, and they're having a lot of fun while doing it.

The second thing that happens when you build a trust floor is that the cost of failure increases. This is both a beautiful and a terrifying thing. There's something deeply healing in sharing so much vulnerability with a person, opening ourselves up to them over a period of time. And, at the same time, the longer we open ourselves up in a relationship, the more potential there is for wounding. We don't have control over how the person we've committed ourselves to is going to act today, or tomorrow, or next week. We have no guarantees. Safety is an illusion.

There's something sacred about the security and fragility coexisting. It reflects the nature of the universe, the nature of faith and spirituality. It's a reminder of the mystery we continue to live within; there are no guarantees. And, when those floors that we have spent years building crumble, the pain is that much greater. Sometimes we can repair after these breaks, and sometimes we can't.

I hate this paradox of safety and risk, because it shows how much we need safety, and it exposes how fragile our relationships are. Practically, we *need* safety. Our relationships are built on trust; we choose our partners, our friends, and the people we surround ourselves with because (usually) they make us feel safe. Our oxytocin and vasopressin build when we're with these people, yet that safety is ultimately an illusion, a complex interaction of chemicals in our brains that can't actually control what another person will do.

But this is also where the beauty of our relationships lies. When we choose to build a trust floor with someone, whether in our friendships, romantic relationships, or our sexual relationships, we can't take that trust floor for granted. We have to appreciate it for what it is, and we must continually choose to remain vulnerable and not close ourselves off. We choose to return again and again, to open ourselves up to being hurt and at the same time open ourselves to being known. It's a dance of pleasure and pain, a dance of coming together and falling apart; it's the dance of life and of relationship. We get things right.

We get things wrong. Trust gets built, and trust gets broken. It's messy, and it's what keeps us going.

Notes

1. Michael J. Bader, *Arousal: The Secret Logic of Sexual Fantasies* (New York: Thomas Dunne, 2002), 18.

CHAPTER 10.

PARADOX 4: WE WILL GET THINGS WRONG AND RIGHT AT THE SAME TIME

When I was seventeen, my family moved to Romania. A few months before my parents announced the move, we had gone on a two-week trip to Romania, visiting a small town just south of the Carpathian Mountains to help a local missionary family remodel a building to use as a space for teaching English classes. Then we were asked to move there.

When my parents told my sisters and me the news, my youngest sister stared at them in shock. "What?! No. We're not going to do that, are we?"

But within two months, we had put our house, small farm, and 90 percent of our belongings up for auction and were on track to become missionaries. First, we traveled to rural Montana for four months of missionary training. Then we made a quick stop back home in Iowa before taking a nearly twenty-four-hour series of flights to Romania, the last place I expected to finish out my high school years.

One of the first things we did was to try to learn Romanian. We took a few classes while still in the United States but told ourselves that once we got to Romania and were immersed, we would pick it up quickly. After all,

Romanian is one of the easiest languages for an English speaker to learn, or so we were told.

That's not what happened. During our first few weeks in the country, we quickly learned some grammar rules, a couple of additional letters in the alphabet, and what they sounded like. We learned the accent marks, how they modify vowels, and a little about sentence structure. By my second month in Romania, I could read the language out loud proficiently, with very few corrections from my new friends who were native speakers.

I felt great, but there was one problem: I had no idea what I was saying. Time after time, my Romanian friends would give me a piece of paper and say, "Here, read this," and burst into laughter, reveling in the fact that my lack of real understanding led me to read some pretty embarrassing sentences out loud.

In our first week of classes, our teacher Elena told us this simple truth: you can learn all the words and rules of a language; you can memorize, memorize, memorize; but you don't truly start learning the language until you practice with other people. Learning a language requires trying to speak it every chance you get, which means making mistakes—lots of mistakes. Memorizing the rules is important, but for a language to become meaningful for us, we have to be willing to make fools of ourselves.

The other missionaries in the village agreed with Elena. Our friend Kimberly, who had moved to Romania from the United States nearly ten years before, told us story after story about the mistakes she made while learning. But now, because of those mistakes, she was flourishing. Kimberly's accent was almost impeccable.

Without a willingness to dive right in and make mistakes, it's impossible to learn any language—or a musical instrument or a new dance, or almost anything else for that matter. All those mistakes feel uncomfortable; you feel like a fool, you're full of shame, and you want to yell, "I promise I'm competent in other areas of my life!"

Coming to terms with our sexuality and creating healthy sex lives is similar to learning a language. Both require witnessing the new mode of communication through experience, correction, and seeing the results of our actions. We will make mistakes, and in the process of making mistakes, we are getting it right. We can spend all our time studying the "rules" and recite them proficiently, but without experience, without the ability to witness another person, we can't really call ourselves fluent.

That's our fourth paradox: we will and we won't get things right. But through the process of making mistakes, through the process of getting it all wrong, we are doing it right.

If you're not sexually active and working on physical expression, you can still be working with your sexuality. I'm not saying you *must* or *should* be sexually active. I'm simply saying that sex and sexuality must be experienced. If waiting to be sexually active feels congruent with your values, then explore your sexuality instead. Work with your own body and the other forms of sexuality that you do want to experience right now. For example, set aside time to masturbate slowly, paying attention to every sensation that comes up and not rushing to reach a climax. You will get things right while doing that, and you will get things wrong, and you will be learning all the while. Know that when you become sexually active, the same back and forth between getting things right and wrong will happen.

Like each of the other paradoxes we've already explored, these truths apply whether we're sexually active or not. This is something that many LGBTQ people understand intuitively. People often ask us, "Well, how do you know you're gay if you've never slept with a person of another gender?" Many of us know well before ever having sex for the first time who we're attracted to, because we've paid attention to the experience of our bodies. We have felt aroused by people of the same gender or reacted negatively when someone of another gender has gone in for a kiss. Sexual experience doesn't translate exclusively to sexual activity.

Of course, it's also true that we learn things through sexual activity that we cannot learn any other way. While many queer people know they're queer way before ever having sex, I have a friend who learned that she was a lesbian only through the experience of getting married to a man and having sex with him. She had waited until marriage to have sex. She thought she was straight, and it was a slow process for her to realize that she actually didn't have any sexual desire for the man she married. This is a tragic experience but one that allowed her to continue to move toward flourishing. She is now in a happy relationship with a woman and still has a great friendship with her ex-husband.

Regardless of where we are, regardless of what we are experiencing, our fourth paradox shows us that getting things wrong is just part of the process. It means we are in it, learning about our bodies, learning what works and doesn't work. If we are actively engaging the sexual parts of ourselves with intentionality and care, however that looks, we are getting it right.

If making mistakes and messing up—also known as getting things "wrong"—ultimately means we're engaging with our sexuality and our sex lives the right way, then our constructs of "right" and "wrong" are turned on their heads, aren't they? The "getting things right and wrong" paradox introduces some fluidity into the equation. It doesn't remove the ideals of right and wrong; cultural norms, laws, and values offer some firm boundaries, particularly when it comes to abuse. But in most scenarios, this paradox does prevent us from assigning moral judgments to our actions. In faith communities especially, we're used to holding our lives up to some sort of moral standard and then determining our worth based on our adherence to that standard. We want a list on paper or big stone tablets that tells us we are good if we do certain things and bad if we do other things. However, this paradox makes it impossible to create such a list, because there is no more rigid divide between right and wrong.

SELF-RIGHTEOUSNESS OR DESPAIR

When we describe ourselves as good or bad based upon how well we are adhering to a code, it is so much easier for shame to jump in and ruin things. If we're existing in this binary, we're usually in one of two positions: either we are self-righteous, telling everyone, "Look at me obeying so well, and look at all these other people who aren't," or we're in a place of despair, saying, "Look at what a terrible person I am, the worst of all sinners." This is the natural result of measuring our worth based on our adherence to strict codes of right and wrong that were created outside ourselves, and this is primarily how we are taught to exist in many faith communities.

Both self-righteousness and despair are places of shame. Despair says, "I'm a terrible person. I can never be good by myself." It is the voice of shame personified, almost a complete overtaking of our identity by shame. Sadly, so much of our theological teaching and theological language encourages this, as if denigrating ourselves somehow makes our faith stronger, as if berating ourselves somehow enhances our connection to God.

Self-righteousness is the other side of the same coin, and it's a protective mechanism rooted in fear of shame. Self-righteousness says, "I must strictly adhere to this code, or else I will be overtaken by my badness. This is the only way I can ensure that I am good." Whenever we try to behave in the "right" way, shame is always lurking, and it is the driving force of a striving after goodness.

Both of these positions are futile, because they keep us stuck in a system that is ultimately boxed in, suffocating, with absolutely no freedom. But there is another way, a different system that has nothing to do with labels like "good" and "bad" but instead is concerned with freedom. Freedom leads to flourishing for all people.

We don't actually have the ability to assign goodness and badness to ourselves or to others. All our attempts to define morality and base our worth upon those definitions will be ineffective. The definitions themselves simply trap us in shame loops. What we think is good can in the long run turn out to be horribly destructive. What we believe is a mistake can turn out to be the exact right thing in the moment. The ultimate determination of these things requires time, experience, and witness. A prime example of this is first dates. So often, I'll go home after a first date and replay the entire conversation in my head, calling myself some choice names and wondering, "What in the world was I thinking, telling that story?!" I have friends who do this, too, who have found out later, once their relationships have been established, that it was those exact stories, those exact quirks that drew their partners to them. It's the stuff of wedding toasts.

Freeing ourselves of our notions of goodness and badness is hard, because it means there are no easy answers to our questions about morality and therefore no easy answers to our questions about sexual ethics. In my experience, the truest answer to most questions about sexual ethics is "Well, it depends . . ." Such questions involve a level of complexity that is erased when we keep pursuing old quests for certainty about right and wrong.

I know it may seem that I'm asking you to do something impossible. We exist in a world that encourages us every day to define ourselves based upon the categories of good and bad, which is a source of shame. When we are able to embrace the fact that making mistakes is an essential part of being human, we can begin to let go of some of that shame. Remember my client Leon from chapter 1? He grew up in rural Texas and lived a double life—a worship leader who spent night after night hooking up with random people. Leon deeply regretted these experiences, especially after he moved to Seattle, came out, and began working through some of the shame he had been holding around his sexuality. He came to see me because of that shame.

Making mistakes is part of our journey toward healthy sexuality. Sexual health does not mean the absence of mistakes; it means learning from our mistakes and letting them guide us as we move forward. Sometimes we realize that what we once called a mistake wasn't actually a mistake at all.

I hear stories all the time about people like Leon who regret sexual decisions they have made. They feel bound to these experiences and describe them as if the experiences destroyed some of their worth, some of their value, because they've done things that don't align with their value systems. They feel deep shame. Eventually, Leon was able to see that he had been coping the only way he knew how. He wasn't in a place where he could integrate his sexuality. He didn't have the tools. Through our work together, Leon was able to gain a different perspective on this part of his life, and he came to see it as a valuable part of his journey toward health.

Any of us can so easily get caught up in these kinds of feelings, too, berating ourselves or shaking our heads and wondering, "What was I thinking?" We can look back on our past selves with hate or disgust. It's one thing to be able to say, "Yeah, sometimes we get things wrong, and sometimes we get things right," but it's another to actually reckon with and learn from the shame that comes when we do things we're not proud of.

WORKING THROUGH SHAME

When we're faced with shame around our sexual decisions (or any choice, for that matter), three steps can help us work through these feelings: (1) recognize the shame; (2) understand the why; and (3) practice self-compassion.

First, and this may seem obvious, we need to recognize when we are having a shame response. It's common in our world to base our worth on how much or how little sex we are having, and shame responses have become part of our natural disposition. We hear our friends talking about the sex they are having after going out, and we automatically compare ourselves and assign value to that, whether positive or negative. If we haven't recognized our shame, then we can't work with it. Shame can move unchecked when it is unrecognized. Naming our shame concretely can be incredibly helpful here: "I am feeling shame because I hooked up with that girl after dancing with her in the club. That felt like a mistake."

Once we name our shame, we can move toward understanding why we did what we did. Quite often, our mistakes are rooted in good intentions or honest emotions. For example, Hannah from chapter 2 broke up with her girlfriend the day after she had sex. Hannah still is not particularly proud of that. The shame she feels about this still occasionally comes up in our work together. But in our sessions, stopping to explore why she did that helps her work with her shame. As we touched on in chapter 7, Hannah slept with her girlfriend because she wanted a deeper connection; she wanted to move their relationship to a deeper level, and she wanted to finally experience a sexual relationship. Those are beautiful things. Hannah can honor those parts of herself that wanted connection, those parts of herself that wanted intimacy, and name those as good. Her desire for connection and intimacy is a good thing. She can simultaneously name those things as good and acknowledge that the outcome wasn't what she wanted.

Naming a deeper why and recognizing what motivated our actions automatically introduces complexity into our shame narratives. Now "I am bad because I slept with that girl and then broke up with her" turns to "I really hoped sleeping with her would help us connect, but it didn't. I regret that." That's a much more honest space. It doesn't remove the reality of hurt in the process, but it does help her see that what she was searching for was something good: connection.

The point here is not to use this more sophisticated understanding of our motivations as an excuse. I can recognize that my intention behind the action was to find a deeper connection and simultaneously see that my impact was hurtful. If the other person were to come to me and say, "You hurt me, and you shouldn't have done that," it would be so easy for me to say, "I didn't mean to. I just wanted to connect with you. I'm sorry you feel hurt." But that's me puffing up to protect myself from the pain we're both feeling; it's not being honest.

Recognizing why we did something doesn't automatically make it OK and absolve us from responsibility. When people tell us that we hurt them, we need to take that seriously, regardless of our intentions. But recognizing our intentions can help keep our shame voices—which serve no helpful purpose—at bay. We are not bad people because we hurt someone, and labeling ourselves as such doesn't solve the problem. After we acknowledge our shame, we can then work to repair the relationship from a place of integrity and compassion: "I didn't mean to hurt you, and I am so sorry that I did."

The final step, after we've named our shame and recognized the why, is to practice self-compassion. To practice self-compassion is simply "to treat ourselves with the same kindness, caring, and compassion we would show to a good friend, or even a stranger for that matter."[1] By identifying all the complexity in ourselves—the fact that we're feeling shame, that we had good intentions, and that we've hurt ourselves and others—and then normalizing that reality, we can move toward self-compassion.

It's so incredibly normal to hurt someone while having good intentions. It happens all the time to every person on the planet. It's also normal to feel bad, and as we recognize that we're living into part of our human experience, we can then choose to offer ourselves kindness. Kindness and compassion don't erase the pain, nor do they absolve us from taking responsibility for the pain we've caused and the people we've hurt, but with the strength gained from compassion, we can begin to repair the relationship. Shame isn't a part of the equation when we do this; instead, we're operating from a grounded place, a place where all the complexity of feelings is recognized and acknowledged.

These three steps I've outlined will free us up to witness reality. Hannah was able to look back at the story of breaking up with her girlfriend and see both the truth that she wanted connection *and* that her quest for connection was ultimately painful for both of them. Does that make her bad or good? Neither. She made choices; some were beneficial, some were painful, but none of those choices reflect who Hannah *is*.

We don't have to be ashamed of our past sexual decisions. We don't have to look at them purely as mistakes.

We don't have to berate ourselves and use them as object lessons. Even if we're not proud of some of the choices we have made, instead of looking back and exclaiming, "What was I thinking?!" merely as a prelude to pronouncing ourselves ruined and shameful, we can answer that question with honesty.

What were we thinking? In most cases, we were probably pursuing connection, love, belonging, goodness, intimacy, and pleasure. Should we blame ourselves for making the choices we made in that moment? Rather than blame ourselves, we can ask whether we have learned something about others and ourselves from the experience. If we were faced with that same situation and that same moment today, we might make a different choice based upon our experience, or we might not.

So far, we've been looking at experiences and choices we regret in some way. We also sometimes may feel an obligation to regret sexual experiences that don't fit what we've been taught is acceptable, even though, when it comes down to it, those experiences were actually pretty amazing and positive. Several months ago, a client who grew up in a conservative Christian environment walked into my office and told me that she had just hooked up with a guy she had no intention of pursuing a relationship with.

"I felt so good in the morning. The sex was amazing!" She was trying to stifle a big smile. "I don't feel bad about it, but I feel like I should." We spent the session unpacking the common message that we have to regret, or feel guilty about, or feel shame about any sexual experience that doesn't fit within traditional narratives. As we explored her experience, we determined that she had acted within the values she had set out for herself. And she had really enjoyed herself. She didn't feel guilty because she had nothing to feel guilty about.

What about when we get things right? For some of us, it can be harder to name and claim getting it "right" than getting it "wrong." We gloss right over these experiences or feel anxiety, wondering, "Should I feel bad about this? Surely that wasn't as good as it seemed." It's much easier to dwell on what we get wrong or tune into the voices that encourage us to find fault in our choices, because the human brain maintains a negativity bias. We are evolutionarily wired to remember our negative experiences. This means our brains automatically gloss over good experiences and favor the negative ones because the more we're able to avoid negative experiences, the better our chances of survival. When we have really good sex, sex that we and our partners enjoy, we can practice letting it simply be good, without placing judgment on it.

In the six months I lived in Romania before moving back to the United States for college, I didn't get much further than learning basic Romanian phrases for daily survival. It was too easy to switch back into English, which most of my Romanian friends were quite happy with, because they could actually understand me, and they could continue to hone their English skills. My friends knew that the right way to learn a language is to make mistakes, but I wasn't willing to get uncomfortable enough to make those mistakes, so I never really learned from the experience.

As we have positive and negative sexual experiences, as we witness ourselves and others in relation to our sexuality, we learn. We learn about ourselves, and we learn about others. We learn what we like and what we don't like. Since we are continually learning, there is no one "right" sexual ethic and no one "right" way to do sexuality. Accepting the fourth paradox—that we will and we won't get it right, sometimes at the same time—encourages us to enjoy our sexuality right now. Whatever values we decide on for ourselves, as we work toward flourishing for ourselves and for others, we can celebrate when we experience it, and we can offer ourselves kindness when we do things that diminish flourishing and then trust ourselves to move back toward flourishing as we continue on our journey.

Notes

1. Kristin Neff, *Self-Compassion: The Proven Power of Being Kind to Yourself* (New York: William Morrow, 2011), 6.

CONCLUSION: THE FINAL PARADOX: EMBRACING SHAME

On a Thursday evening a few years ago, I left a public lecture at a local university to grab a drink of water. At the drinking fountain, I ran into a few friends I hadn't seen in months. As we chatted, I caught the gaze of an absolutely beautiful man I had never seen before and held eye contact.

Much to my horror, he immediately altered his path to the restroom and walked straight up to us, interrupting our conversation, looking directly at me. "Hi, I'm James," he said with a big smile. "I think I saw you on Tinder a few weeks ago?"

I didn't remember, but I was smitten, my heart fluttering. I stumbled through an introduction, and we exchanged numbers with the plan of grabbing drinks later that evening. Then I went back to sit with my friend Aubrey in the lecture hall.

"I think I just met my husband," I said to her.

We did meet up that night and talked until two in the morning, leaving only because the bar was closing. The next weekend, James and I spent almost every moment we could getting to know each other. On Saturday afternoon, a huge snowstorm hit Seattle.

"Why don't you come back to my place to wait out the

storm? It's close," James suggested, with a sly smile on his face.

We were pretty far from my apartment, and the roads were already icy. In that moment, I had a choice to make: brave the slippery roads and go home, turning away from the invitation to sex that was the subtext of James's invitation, or go back to James's place and face my sexuality with my mom's voice whispering, "Cover your eyes, Matt," in my head.

It wasn't a hard decision. In fact, I had been hoping the weekend would lead to this. Minutes later, we were in James's apartment, kissing and undressing. I'll spare you the details but highlight the connection that was made between us momentarily that afternoon.

THE POWER OF CONNECTION

When I first started researching sexual ethics, I stumbled across a short essay by the theologian Rowan Williams. That essay, titled "The Body's Grace," to this day remains one of the most poignant pieces I have ever read about sex and sexuality. In it, Williams wonders if the big question around sexual morality is this: "How much do we want our sexual activity to communicate? How much do we want it to display a breadth of human possibility and a sense of the body's capacity to heal and enlarge the life of others?"[1] For Williams, the marker of a moral sexual relationship is not our adherence to a list of rules of what is and what isn't acceptable; instead, the measure is what we are communicating with our bodies. Are we expanding connection and flourishing, or are we diminishing connection?

All sexual relationships, whether they are momentary or long-term, have the potential to move us toward expansion and connection, toward flourishing, toward the integration of our shame. They also have the potential to move us away from all of these things into avoidance and dis-integration. It's all based on how we connect or don't connect and on how we then work with ourselves and the people we are with when disconnection is inevitable. I agree with Williams that the ideal is ultimately finding a person, or people, to share in a long-term vulnerable, developing relationship. Shame gets fought more fully in these kinds of relationships, because we're able to work with that shame over a long period of time, and as more gets uncovered, we get to deeper layers. But I also believe that people can come alongside us and help us with our shame in a variety of different ways, including short-term relationships.

Let me apply this to my weekend with James. Later that Saturday evening, James and I braved the snow to grab dinner, and I caught a glimpse of myself in the mirror. I couldn't quite comprehend what I was seeing: I looked like a different person. Maybe it was the restaurant lighting, but I barely recognized myself. The man I was looking at—myself—was radiant, with piercing blue eyes. Instead of being greeted by the shame that sometimes comes with a glance in the mirror, I was seeing myself the way James saw me that weekend.

This story illustrates my point. By turning toward James, by turning toward my own sexuality that afternoon, I experienced a new kind of connection firsthand. Through witnessing his desire for me and my desire for him, I was able to see myself in a different way.

Something had shifted in me in that encounter. Some of my shame was gone.

EMBRACING CONNECTION

My mom tells me that as a toddler, my favorite book was *The Little Engine That Could.* Before bed, I would run up to her, holding the book out, whispering, "I tink I can, I tink I can, I tink I can."

The book is a classic—the story of a little train engine that has a long string of heavy cars to carry. She travels along, moving forward with some exertion but relative ease until she comes to a great big hill. The train looks up the hill with trepidation but decides to try to scale it by herself. She chugs and chugs, but no matter how hard the little engine tries, the weight is too heavy, and she can't get up the track.

So she starts to look for help. She asks a couple of larger engines to help her carry the load, but each of them declines her offer with excuses like "I've already been cleaned and don't want to get dirty helping you" and "I'm too important to help little engines" and "I'm too tired." She begins to get discouraged, but just when she's about to lose all hope of climbing the mountain, she sees another little engine that looks just like her.

"Will you help me?" the little engine asks. They look at her load together, somewhat skeptically, and the other little engine says, "Well, I can try!"

The engines link together and begin their trek up the hill, chanting to themselves, "I think I can, I think I can, I think I can!" They strain and pull, chanting all the way, "I think I can, I think I can, I think I can," and slowly but surely, they work their way up the hill. And they make it, together.

The book ends with the two engines saying good-bye and the little engine continuing on her way, now whispering, "I thought I could, I thought I could, I thought I could," all the way into the distance. I imagine that her load felt a little bit lighter.

When it comes to sexual shame, and shame in general, we're like that little engine. We plug along, doing the best that we can, carrying heavy weight with us, but eventually we come across a hill, and that shame feels insurmountable. We try to find different ways of climbing the hill—our coping mechanisms. Some of us hide from the hill, avoid the hill, or try to find ways around the hill. Others of us try to muscle our way up the hill, ignore it, or pretend everything is fine, all the while yelling breathlessly, "What hill?! You're the one trying to climb a hill, not me! No hill here!" Others of us try to climb the hill occasionally but find that we're actually pretty content just camping out at the base, promising that we'll deal with it eventually but forgetting about it in the meantime. None of these approaches actually gets us up the hill. Instead, we're left with our huge weight, looking around, trying to figure out how in the world we're going to make it.

So we talk about fighting shame, getting rid of it, working with ourselves to lighten the weight. And in some ways, that works. We can let a couple of cars go, alleviating the burden a little bit. Still, we find that no matter how hard we work, the weight doesn't disappear, and we still can't get up the hill.

I think that's where we might be right now, staring up at that big hill, wondering how in the world we are going to face it. We've explored the hill and the ways we try to cope with the reality of it. We've looked back at the weight we're carrying, and we've worked to understand some of how it got there and why we're holding it, but we haven't actually climbed the hill. We haven't actually dealt with our shame.

A few weeks ago, I was describing this book to a colleague at the small grad school where I'm an assistant instructor. I told her I'm exploring how we fight sexual shame so we can embrace healthy sexuality. A knowing smile came over her face, and I knew she was about to say something profound.

"We don't fight shame, we embrace it."

Of course, I thought. *That's it. That's what I've been trying to say all along, but I didn't know it.*

We can spend our lives fighting our shame, but ultimately fighting the reality of our shame is like the little engine trying to fight the hill. It's not gonna work. The hill doesn't magically go away, no matter how hard we try to fight it. The only way the little engine was able to get over her hill was to embrace it. This may be the ultimate paradox, our fifth and most important paradox: to get beyond shame, we have to embrace it. Embracing our shame can empower us if we see the connections it offers to other people and to ourselves.

This is a paradox we know well because it shows up throughout our lives. *The only way out is through.* The little engine can do all the work she wants before climbing the hill. She can look at maps, she can read all about it, she can research the hell out of it. But eventually, she's actually going to have to face the hill.

And she can't face it alone.

EMBRACING SHAME

All the way back in the introduction to this book, one of the ways I defined shame was the fear of disconnection. It is the voices both inside and outside of us that convince us we are not worthy of connection because of who we are or what we have done. Shame is anything that attempts to convince us that we are disqualified from connection, whether internal connection (i.e., integrating pieces of ourselves), connection with other people, or connection with God. Because of how closely tied our sexuality is to our personhood, sexuality is a place in our lives where we feel shame most acutely, and it is a place where some of the most shaming messages occur.

The little engine faced a lot of those shaming messages

from other engines that looked like they had everything figured out. The big, smart, important engines refused to help the little engine. Instead, they cut her down: "Who do you think you are? Can't you see we're busy being important? Get with the program."

These engines remind me of those who only heap more burdens upon those of us who are searching for ways to manage and deal with our sexual shame. Instead of helping us pick up the load and get up the hill, they leave us stranded and thinking that *we're* the bad ones. Their messages are ineffective and only serve to make things worse.

Do you see where I'm going with this? The little engine found another little engine, just like her, who was willing to face the challenge alongside her. And even though it took a whole lot of work, they scaled the hill together.

That's the key here. If shame is the fear of disconnection, the way we work with our own shame is by embracing connection. That's what I did with James.

So let's talk about what it means to embrace our shame. After all, shame isn't something we can just say no to. As we've explored, ignoring shame or denying it doesn't make it magically disappear. Framing shame (or anything in our past) as "just a story we tell ourselves" and claiming that it doesn't have power over us is a misunderstanding of reality that only serves to disconnect us from the parts of ourselves that are feeling the shame.

Imagine a fight you've recently been in. If you can't think of a fight you've been in, think of the last fight you've watched on TV or in a movie. Any kind of fight will work, whether it is verbal or physical. When it comes right down to it, fighting is typically an act of disconnection, or dis-integration. It is two or more people, ideas, or groups of people coming into conflict. When we—instead of doing the hard work of understanding the conflict, instead of doing the work of integration—choose to push away from each other, the result is a fight.

When we fight, our most common reaction is to harden up, to dig in our heels, to assert our goals as the most important; we seek to win at all costs. The same is true when we try to fight parts of ourselves. Instead of listening to those parts, instead of seeking to understand why they are there, instead of working to integrate them into ourselves, we push those parts away. Yet as we've explored, that doesn't actually work.

How do we resolve conflict? How do we heal after fights? We reconnect. To embrace our shame, we have to embrace connection. We find other people who will get into the nitty-gritty of our shame with us, who will help us embrace the parts of ourselves that we are scared nobody will love, and we climb those hills together.

Sexuality is uniquely positioned to help us with this task because, as we have established, sex is literally, biologically, about connection. Very few other things connect us in the ways sex connects us. Thus, having sex can be an integral part of helping ourselves get up and over our hills of shame.

Yet, as we've also explored, where there is immense potential for connection, there is also tremendous potential for disconnection. I'm talking about both interpersonal sexuality and our internal sex lives. Are we making choices with our bodies that lead us toward further connection or further disconnection?

You'll notice I've been cautious in this book to avoid prescribing a certain sexual ethic, because the question of connection and disconnection is a question that only *you* can answer for yourself. It looks different for all of us because while we all have common chemicals coursing through our bodies, each of us is unique and responds differently. Our unique sexual ethic is something we have to witness within ourselves.

Each of the four paradoxes in this book serves as a guidepost as we work to evaluate our sex lives and build our sexual ethics. As we pursue sexual health, are we also aware of the risks involved? When we're jumping into bed with someone, are we embracing vulnerability, or are we using sex to avoid vulnerability? If we're using it to avoid vulnerability, are we aware of that and cognizant that eventually the things we're avoiding will have to be faced? Are we using safer sexual practices? Have we built a trust floor? If we don't have a trust floor, how are we going to work with the feelings that might pop up after our dopamine goes away? If we're considering building a trust floor with someone, are we aware of how much more things may hurt if that trust floor gets broken? Are we willing to make mistakes—and in the process get a lot of things right?

Our answers to these questions can lead us closer to—or further away from—connection with other people. Understanding our answers and the way they intersect with our own lives helps us move with intention. Instead of floundering around, we can build principles and practices that are good for us and kind to ourselves—practices that allow us to use our voice, explore our bodies, work toward mutual pleasure, and ultimately help heal shame in our lives.

EMBRACING ENDINGS

I think one of the most beautiful things about the *Little Engine That Could* is that the engine who helped her up the hill says good-bye before the end of the story. They don't chug off into the distance together, living happily ever after, carrying the load. And while that ending to the story would be just as beautiful, it doesn't feel as realistic to me.

You may dream of finding that one special person to live happily ever after with, and while this is certainly a possibility, I also think it's vital that we reckon with the fact that relationships end. Sometimes people come into our lives for a season; they help us up a hill or two, and then they leave us.

While I believe lasting, committed relationships are possible, and also necessary. (There's something that happens to us when we commit to people, whether in friendships, long-term relationships, or marriages. People can add to or help take away our shame based on how we connect with them.) The brutal reality is that relationships end—sometimes no matter how hard we try. So this is another thing we have to hold with complexity.

My relationship with James didn't last very long, yet the changes in myself did. I was more connected to my body, I was more confident in myself, and James had helped teach me I was *worth* that kind of connection. Even though things with James ended, what I experienced with him is not something I would give up. Parts of me were truly transformed though my brief relationship with him. I see this happen with my friends and in my clients often. It can happen with all of us.

Some of us will say good-bye more often than others, depending on how we decide we want to live out our sexual ethics. I would imagine that after the other little engine chugged away, the Little Engine's load felt simultaneously heavier and lighter at the same time. It felt heavier because she had to bear it all by herself again, but lighter and more bearable because another engine had been willing to get into the mess of her journey with her.

When we embrace connection and vulnerability, when we're in spaces that promote safety and integration, something happens to our shame. It doesn't magically just go away, but as we continue to move forward in our relationships and build trust, as those we trust embrace the hidden parts of us, we change. As shame is embraced, it begins to lose its power. We begin to see ourselves more clearly, with new eyes. We begin to see how radiant we actually are.

If shame is about disconnection, then the antidote is connection. When we connect and integrate those parts of ourselves that we feel shame around, we build resilience. Some of that work we can do ourselves, through practices like self-compassion and mindfulness. But most of that work takes other people—people who can embrace us in tangible ways. Sometimes that embrace can happen in a single moment. Like my experience with James, we can all have experiences with people that completely shift our internal worlds. Sometimes it can take a lifetime, a continual choosing into connection. As that happens, we slowly open up more and more of ourselves to the embrace of connection. If we turn toward our sexual relationships with this understanding, they become an incredibly powerful tool to help us move beyond shame.

CLIMBING OUR HILLS TOGETHER

The Little Engine That Could needed help to be able to climb the big hill. I needed James to help me climb one of my hills that afternoon in his apartment. We all need help climbing our hills and finding connection. We have to open ourselves up to connect and let others connect with us. As we embrace each other, we embrace each other's shame and transform it.

The beauty here is that the paradoxes we have been exploring are true about every single relationship we ever encounter, not just sexual ones. We can practice the intentionality these paradoxes invite us into with anyone—in our friendships or with the stranger sitting next to us on a plane. These paradoxes give us a road map to connection, and whether we practice that connection while being intimate in our bedrooms, with ourselves by exploring our bodies, or simply over coffee with a dear friend, each time we turn toward connection, we turn toward an embrace of our shame. And we move beyond it.

Here's my final call to you: don't cover your eyes. Open them wide and look around. Look around at the people who surround you, at all your relationships, and embrace what they bring to you in all their complexity. Look at the health, the safety, and the risk. Despite your feelings of vulnerability and avoidance, turn toward these things. Turn toward one of the most powerful tools you have for connection: your sexuality. Whether with other people or by yourself, turn toward connection.

Moving beyond shame is a practice. It's a task that takes a high level of commitment, a high level of intention, and it can feel daunting. But the wonderful part about turning toward our sexuality is that it's usually pretty enjoyable if we're engaging in it in a way that is consistent with our values. It's up to us to put these principles into practice, to choose to use our sexuality in ways that connect, and to work with ourselves to connect the parts of ourselves that feel shame when we don't. It's not easy work. But can we do it?

Like the Little Engine, I think we can.

And maybe it's time to make a few mistakes.

Notes

1. Rowan Williams, "The Body's Grace," in *Our Selves, Our Souls and Bodies: Sexuality and the Household of God*, ed. Charles Hefling (Boston: Cowley, 1996), 61.

RESOURCES AND FURTHER READING

The following lists recommend resources related to various themes and topics raised in the chapters. These lists are not exhaustive but are good starting points. Some resources are listed more than once because they fit in multiple categories.

SHAME, COGNITION, AND EMOTION

Brown, Brené. *Daring Greatly: How the Courage to Be Vulnerable Transforms the Way We Live, Love, Parent, and Lead.* New York: Avery, 2012.

Brown, Brené. *The Gifts of Imperfection: Let Go of Who You Think You're Supposed to Be and Embrace Who You Are.* Center City, MN: Hazelden, 2010.

Damasio, Antonio. *Descartes' Error: Emotion, Reason, and the Human Brain.* New York: Penguin, 2005.

Damasio, Antonio. *The Feeling of What Happens: Body and Emotion in the Making of Consciousness.* New York: Mariner, 2000.

Siegel, Daniel J. *Mindsight: The New Science of Personal Transformation.* New York: Bantam, 2011.

Thompson, Curt. *The Soul of Shame: Retelling the Stories We Believe about Ourselves.* Downers Grove, IL: InterVarsity, 2015.

PATRIARCHY AND PURITY CULTURE: PERSPECTIVES FROM WOMEN

Anderson, Dianna. *Damaged Goods: New Perspectives on Christian Purity.* New York: Jericho, 2015.

Bessey, Sarah. *Jesus Feminist: An Invitation to Revisit the Bible's View of Women.* New York: Howard, 2013.

Bolz-Weber, Nadia. *Shameless: A Sexual Reformation.* New York: Convergent, 2019.

brown, adrienne maree. *Pleasure Activism: The Politics of Feeling Good.* Chico, CA: AK Press, 2019.

Farley, Margaret. *Just Love: A Framework for Christian Sexual Ethics.* New York: Continuum, 2006.

Finch, Jamie Lee. *You Are Your Own: A Reckoning with the Religious Trauma of Evangelical Christianity.* Self-published, 2019.

Gilligan, Carol. *The Birth of Pleasure: A New Map of Love.* New York: Vintage, 2003.

Gilligan, Carol, and David A. J. Richards. *Darkness Now Visible: Patriarchy's Resurgence and Feminist Resistance.* New York: Cambridge University Press, 2018.

Gonzalez, Michelle A. *Created in God's Image: An Introduction to Feminist Theological Anthropology.* Maryknoll, NY: Orbis, 2007.

Griffith, R. Marie. *Moral Combat: How Sex Divided American Christians and Fractured American Politics.* New York: Basic, 2017.

Henderson-Espinoza, Robyn. *Activist Theology.* Minneapolis: Fortress, 2019.

hooks, bell. *Feminism Is for Everybody: Passionate Politics.* New York: Routledge, 2015.

Joy, Emily. www.emilyjoypoetry.com.

Klein, Linda Kay. *Pure: Inside the Evangelical Movement That Shamed a Generation of Young Women and How I Broke Free.* New York: Touchstone, 2018.

Kwok, Pui-lan. *Postcolonial Imagination and Feminist Theology.* Louisville: Westminster John Knox, 2005.

Lerner, Gerda. *The Creation of Patriarchy.* New York: Oxford University Press, 1986.

McCleneghan, Bromleigh. *Good Christian Sex: Why Chastity Isn't the Only Option—and Other Things the Bible Says about Sex.* New York: HarperOne, 2016.

The Mystic Soul Project. www.mysticsoulproject.com.

Nagoski, Emily. *Come as You Are: The Surprising New Science That Will Transform Your Sex Life.* New York: Simon & Schuster, 2015.

Sellers, Tina Schermer. *Sex, God, and the Conservative Church: Erasing Shame from Sexual Intimacy.* New York: Routledge, 2017.

Taylor, Keeanga-Yamahtta, ed. *How We Get Free: Black Feminism and the Combahee River Collective.* Chicago: Haymarket, 2017.

Valenti, Jessica. *The Purity Myth: How America's Obsession with Virginity Is Hurting Young Women.* Berkeley, CA: Seal, 2010.

Velasco-Sanchez, AnaYelsi. "This Land Is Our Land? On Being IndoLatinx at a Women's March." *Bienvenidos* (blog), January 26, 2017. https://tinyurl.com/y4j7knmq.

THE BIBLE, SEXUALITY, AND GENDER

Baldock, Kathy. *Walking the Bridgeless Canyon: Repairing the Breach between the Church and the LGBT Community.* Reno, NV: Canyonwalker, 2014.

Brownson, James V. *Bible, Gender, Sexuality: Reframing the Church's Debate on Same-Sex Relationships.* Grand Rapids: Eerdmans, 2013.

DeFranza, Megan K. *Sex Difference in Christian Theology: Male, Female, and Intersex in the Image of God.* Grand Rapids: Eerdmans, 2015.

Edman, Elizabeth M. *Queer Virtue: What LGBTQ People Know*

About Life and Love and How It Can Revitalize Christianity. Boston: Beacon Press, 2016.

Hartke, Austen. *Transforming: The Bible and the Lives of Transgender Christians.* Louisville: Westminster John Knox, 2018.

Keen, Karen R. *Scripture, Ethics, and the Possibility of Same-Sex Relationships.* Grand Rapids: Eerdmans, 2018.

Kegler, Emmy. *One Coin Found: How God's Love Stretches to the Margins.* Minneapolis: Fortress, 2019.

Martin, Colby. *UnClobber: Rethinking Our Misuse of the Bible on Homosexuality.* Louisville: Westminster John Knox, 2016.

Trible, Phyllis. *God and the Rhetoric of Sexuality (Overtures to Biblical Theology).* Philadelphia: Fortress, 1978.

Vines, Matthew. *God and the Gay Christian: The Biblical Case in Support of Same-Sex Relationships.* New York: Convergent, 2014.

THE SCIENCE OF SEXUALITY

Breuning, Loretta Graziano. *Habits of a Happy Brain: Retrain Your Brain to Boost Your Serotonin, Dopamine, Oxytocin, and Endorphin Levels.* Avon, MA: Adams, 2016.

Fisher, Helen. *Why We Love: The Nature and Chemistry of Romantic Love.* New York: Henry Holt, 2004.

Freitas, Donna. *The End of Sex: How Hookup Culture Is Leaving a Generation Unhappy, Sexually Unfulfilled, and Confused about Intimacy.* New York: Basic, 2013.

Mucha, Laura. *Love Factually: The Science of Who, How and Why We Love.* London: Bloomsbury, 2019.

Nagoski, Emily. *Come as You Are: The Surprising New Science That Will Transform Your Sex Life.* New York: Simon & Schuster, 2015.

Perel, Esther. *Mating in Captivity: Unlocking Erotic Intelligence.* New York: HarperCollins, 2006.

Sukel, Kayt. *This Is Your Brain on Sex: The Science behind the Search for Love.* New York: Simon & Schuster, 2013.

HELP FOR FEELING SAFE WITH OURSELVES

Gunsaullus, Jennifer. "Meditative and Mindful Masturbation for Women." Audio recording. 10 min. www.drjennsden.com /meditative-masturbation.

Neff, Kristin. *Self-Compassion: The Proven Power of Being Kind to Yourself.* New York: William Morrow, 2011.

Siegel, Daniel J. *Aware: The Science and Practice of Presence.* New York: TarcherPerigee, 2018.

SAFER SEX AND SEX EDUCATION RESOURCES

Abrams, Mere. "LGBTQIA Safe Sex Guide." Medically reviewed by Janet Brito. *Healthline*, July 12, 2018. www.health line.com/health/lgbtqia-safe-sex-guide.

American Association of Sexuality Educators, Counselors, and Therapists. www.aasect.org. (Helpful for finding a certified sex-therapist.)

Centers for Disease Control and Prevention (CDC). "Get Tested: National HIV, STD, and Hepatitis Testing." www.gettested.cdc.gov. (Helpful for finding a testing center.)

Corinna, Heather. *S.E.X.: The All-You-Need-to-Know Sexuality Guide to Get through Your Teens and Twenties.* 2nd ed. Philadelphia: Da Capo, 2016.

Haug, Kara. "Grace Unbound." Faith-based sex education. www.graceunbound.com.

Kaufman, Miriam, Cory Silverberg, and Fran Odette. *The Ultimate Guide to Sex and Disability: For All of Us Who Live with Disabilities, Chronic Pain, and Illness.* 2nd ed. San Francisco, CA: Cleis, 2007.

Northwest Institute on Intimacy. Directory for Certified Integrated Intimacy Professionals (CIIP). www.nwioi.com.

Our Whole Lives. United Church of Christ and Unitarian Universalist Association, 2000–09. Comprehensive sex education curriculum for use in churches. www.ucc.org/justice_sexuality-education_our-whole-lives.

WORKING WITH SHAME, SEXUAL SHAME, AND SELF-COMPASSION

Bolz-Weber, Nadia. *Shameless: A Sexual Reformation.* New York: Convergent, 2019.

Brown, Brené. *Rising Strong: How the Ability to Reset Transforms the Way We Live, Love, Parent, and Lead.* New York: Random House, 2017.

Germer, Christopher K. *The Mindful Path to Self-Compassion: Freeing Yourself from Destructive Thoughts and Emotions.* New York: Guilford, 2009.

Hanson, Rick, *Resilient: How to Grow an Unshakable Core of Calm, Strength, and Happiness.* New York: Harmony, 2018.

Neff, Kristin. *Self-Compassion: The Proven Power of Being Kind to Yourself.* New York: William Morrow, 2011.

Sellers, Tina Schermer. *Sex, God, and the Conservative Church: Erasing Shame from Sexual Intimacy.* New York: Routledge, 2017.

ACKNOWLEDGMENTS

The old adage "It takes a village" rings true. And I've probably forgotten some villagers, despite trying to keep a list of every person who helped me along the way.

Dr. Kj Swanson, thank you for helping me tackle this project when it was still a little baby. Thanks for all your notes, critique, perspective, and shaping. Your hands are all over this work.

Speaking of Dr. Swanson, to the students in Dr. Swanson's class God, Gender, and Sexuality at The Seattle School of Theology and Psychology: thank you for letting me workshop this book with you all and for all your conversation, which stimulated further thinking.

Dr. Angela Parker and Dr. Chelle Stearns, the seeds for this book were planted in the year we spent together crafting my thesis. Thank you both for being such incredible academic advisors and for constantly challenging my thinking.

Dr. O'Donnell Day, thank you for putting into language the big aha moment I had been looking for. You've shaped my mind in so many ways.

Dr. Dan Allender, thank you for continually sparking thoughts about sex, sexuality, and shame. Thank you also for your wisdom, kindness, and all your encouragement during the writing process.

Corey Pigg, thank you for helping me navigate the

world of contracts and rights. I couldn't have done this without you.

Shelley Sperry, my goodness, you took this book to another level. Thank you for your structural expertise, your encouragement, and your hours and hours of work on my manuscript.

Lisa Kloskin, my editor, thank you for believing in me from the beginning, for giving me a chance, and for advocating on my behalf. I'm so grateful for your expertise and encouragement.

The entire team at Fortress Press, thank you for all your work to make this book a success. And THANK YOU for publishing queer faith voices!

Charis and Ryan, thank you for that night in the kitchen when we drank wine and read out loud the entire proposal and sample chapters for what became this book. You lit the first sparks that I was onto something.

Gabes Torres, Kellye Kuh, and Annie Mesaros, thank you for helping me shape the outline of this book and for combing through the first draft of the proposal. Also, thanks for putting together my book-deal party. That was so much fun.

Jennifer Fernandez, Charis Santiago, and Tamasin Thomas, thank you for being first readers and for your friendship. You've shaped this book beyond simply offering me your expertise and experience. I am better because of you.

Riley, Pio, Matthew, Daniel, Ryan, Alejandro, Andrew, and Joshua: #AllStars.

Lizz Weaver, Kyle Dyer, and Vicky Beeching, thanks for lending your eyes to cover stuff.

Dr. Tina Schermer Sellers, thank you for believing in this project and for writing such a beautiful foreword.

Lauren Sawyer, Alejandra Morris, Bethany Bylsma, and

Alex Zarecki, thank you for our conversations and the clarification you brought.

Jeremiah Stanley, I'm so lucky to have a friend like you. Thank you for being excited with me, for taking my late-night calls, for sitting with my tears and my complaints, for encouraging me to stand up for myself and stay within my values, for reminding me who I am, and for the billion texts. I will forever cherish the *Book of Well Wishes* you made.

Speaking of the *Book of Well Wishes*, Julie Rodgers, Austen Hartke, Julie Dennis, Trey Pearson, Myles Markham, Matthew Vines, Kenji Kuramitsu, Stacie Burley, Vicky Beeching, Sarah Heath, Abi Robins, Kevin Garcia, and Sarah and Stacey Kessler, thank you for the incredibly encouraging words that you sent Jeremiah. I returned to your notes again and again and again throughout this process. They kept me going.

Sarah and Stacey Kessler, thank you for coaching me through my procrastination and for your encouraging calls and texts. Hopefully, I can come see you more often again, now that this is done.

Kevin Garcia, I'll ask you the same question you never stopped asking me: "Boo, are you working on your book?!" ILYSM.

To the Dream Team, Abi Robins and Stacie Burley: From Arkansas to here, look at us. We're doing it.

Kelsey Leonard, I'm so grateful for your gentle support over the last six years of coffee and brunch.

Thanks also to my dear friends Rachael Clinton, Matt Morrissey, Kalee Vandegrift, Cathy Loerzel, Trapper Lukaart, and everyone at the Allender Center who has offered friendship, guidance, and wisdom and has invited me to take up more space and shine brightly.

Solomon, my therapist, the last six years have been so

much work, but I'm so thankful. This book wouldn't have gotten done without all your support and counsel.

Dad and Mom, thank you for your love in the ways you know how to show it. You raised me well, with kindness and generosity, and I'm thankful for your examples of how to live life with grace. May you discover the more expansive love of Jesus. To my sisters: Mikayla and Anna, thanks for always being there for me.

To my other "parents": Laurie and Stan, Kirk and Amy, Linda and Rob, and Megan, thank you for all your support, for dreaming on my behalf, and for your beautiful care.

To my pastor, Gail Song Bantum: you have changed the game for me. Thank you for letting me approach Quest with every bone of hesitation, for seeing the complexity in what it means for a queer person to walk back into church, for your enthusiasm, and for the ways you challenge me. Let's goooooo.

To Emmy Kegler, Sam Lamott, Jen Hatmaker, Kristen Howerton, Vicky Beeching, Brandan Robertson, Dave and Tino Khalaf, Craig Detweiler, Nadia Bolz-Weber, and Matthew Vines: thank you for the texts, conversations, support, advice, celebration, and shared drinks as I navigated different stages of this process. Knowing I was surrounded by people who have walked this road before and alongside me has been so grounding.

Ariana Grande, ayokay, Beyoncé, Katie Herzig, Billie Eilish, Trevor Hall, Nichole Nordeman, Stasney Mav, Audrey Assad, Troye Sivan, and Sixpence None the Richer, thank you for providing the soundtrack I needed to write. If any of you read this, let's be friends in real life, OK? OK.

And finally, to everyone who listens to and supports me and my podcast *Queerology*, especially those who support my work on Patreon. Thank you for bearing with me as I took unannounced breaks and skipped weeks in order to get this book done. Your emails, financial support, and continual encouragement make what I do possible. Thank you.